I0813341

Let me fall again to prayer and praise.

William Wilberforce
(1759–1833)

Joy of Heaven

Prayers *of the* Revivals

Robert Elmer, Editor

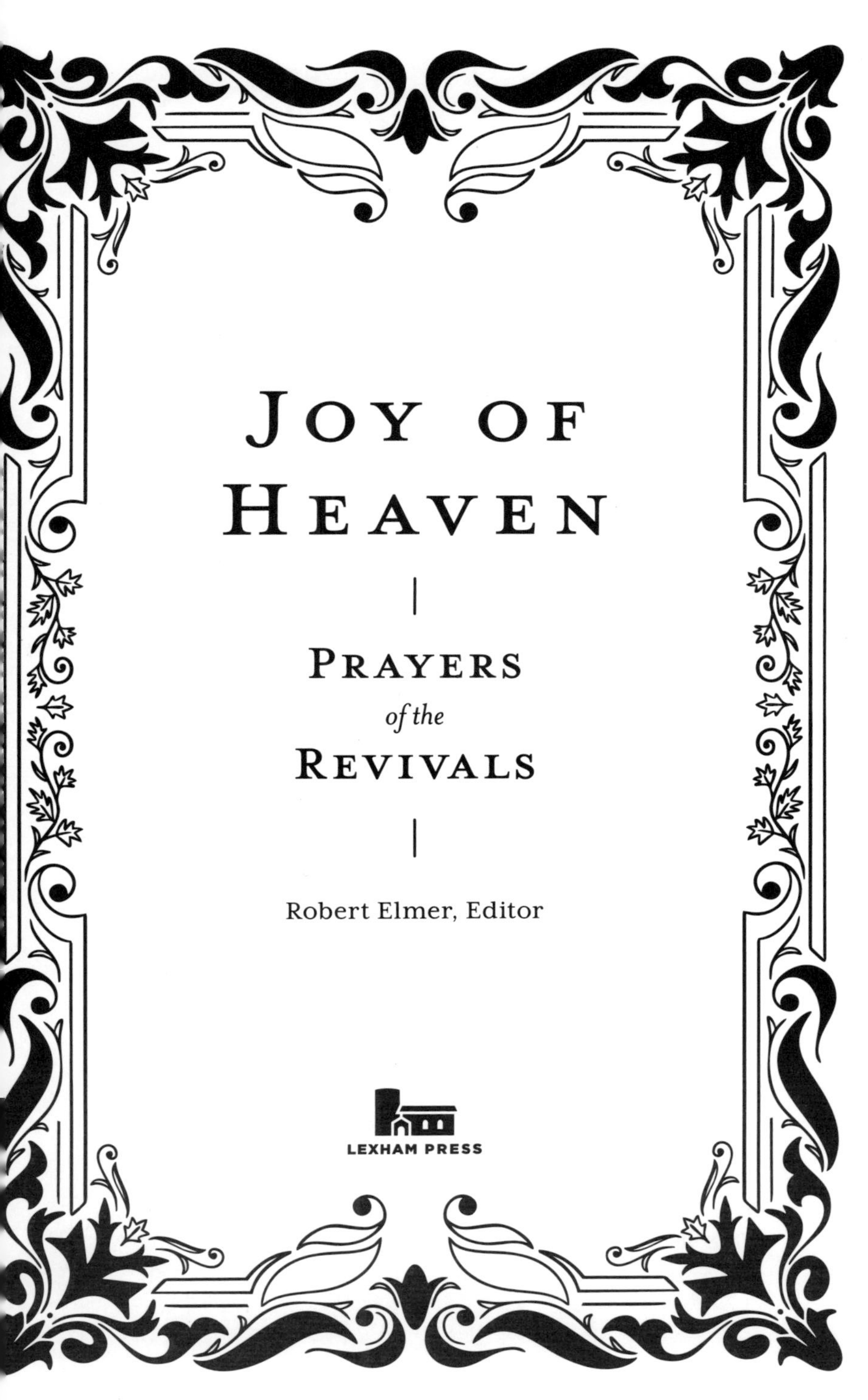

Joy of Heaven

Prayers of the Revivals

Robert Elmer, Editor

LEXHAM PRESS

Joy of Heaven: Prayers of the Revivals
Prayers of the Church, edited by Robert Elmer

Lexham Press, 1313 Bay St., Bellingham, WA 98225
LexhamPress.com

Print ISBN 9781683598626
Digital ISBN 9781683598619
Library of Congress Control Number 2025935884

Lexham Editorial: Elliot Ritzema, Danielle Burlaga, Erin Mangum
Jessi Strong, Mandi Newell
Cover Design: Sarah Brossow
Typesetting: Abigail Stocker

25 26 27 28 29 30 31 / IN / 12 11 10 9 8 7 6 5 4 3 2 1

Introduction

This is a book about discovery.

We're going to discover in these pages how an era of wide-reaching revivals throughout the English-speaking world—awakenings, if you will—have impacted the way we worship today. Covering a span roughly from the early 1700s to around 1925, this era gave rise to many dedicated believers who publicly lived out their faith in Jesus Christ in a rapidly changing world.

And oh how they prayed!

For better or (occasionally) for worse, the lives and examples of these believers cast a greater shadow of influence upon our faith than we may realize. God used these pioneering men and women in powerful ways.

During this time, men like the Wesley brothers, Charles Spurgeon, and A. B. Simpson shared an infectious passion for the Lord that would spread far beyond their pulpits—and lifespans. They prayed fervently for a world that needed Jesus. They prayed for a revival of Bible-believing faith.

At the same time, women like Maria Stewart, Susannah Spurgeon, and Evangeline Booth stood up with great courage to challenge their generation in ways that had never before been witnessed. By listening in on their prayers, we catch a glimpse of their passionate heart for God.

And of course there are many others, often not generally remembered as revivalists per se, but nonetheless equally dedicated to sharing the gospel faith with anyone who would listen (or with anyone who would read their writings). They too prayed for revival, in the broadest sense of the word. We include their powerful prayers in this collection as well.

The decisions these people made and the faith they demonstrated led to new denominations and enduring worship styles. To mass evangelism campaigns and global missionary efforts. To ways of thinking and worshiping and studying the Scriptures that many take for granted today, and that we may slip into as casually as a pair of comfortable Sunday shoes.

These are our spiritual grandparents—people whose faith and ministry significantly (and often spectacularly) touched the course of history. But what did these people believe was most essential on their spiritual journey? What was uppermost in their minds? One of the best ways to find out is to dive into their prayers.

The good news is that archives are full of written prayers from this time, in books and pamphlets, sermons and recorded talks. This was, after all, an era when accessible print media came into its own. Even so, many of the prayers were hidden for decades, largely forgotten and waiting to be rediscovered.

Simply reading the prayers, however, is only a first step. On one level, we may satisfy a curiosity about our spiritual genealogy, if we're inclined to wonder, but a larger part of this journey of discovery is the opportunity these prayers provide to dig deeper into our own relationship with God.

So as with the three previous volumes in the "Prayers of the Church" series, in this collection we will again aim to build a devotional framework from the wisdom and experience of believers who have gone before. If we know how these people prayed, and if we take the opportunity to sincerely adopt their prayers as our own, we build a stronger connection to the past—as well as to the Lord who spans the centuries.

In this way, we can better understand why these people put so much weight on holy living, on seeking God in his word, and on sharing their faith. This realization is our privilege—our birthright, even—as spiritual grandchildren of these men and women. Through these prayers, we have a fresh opportunity to share and live more deeply into the "faith that was once for all delivered to the saints" (Jude 3).

And surely *that* is a discovery well worth making.

—Robert Elmer

List of Authors

Benjamin Allen (1789–1829)

Richard Allen (1760–1831)

Francis Asbury (1745–1816)

Clara Lucas Balfour (1808–1878)

Catherine Booth (1829–1890)

Evangeline Booth (1865–1950)

Amy Carmichael (1867–1951)

Thomas Chalmers (1780–1847)

Penelope Coke (1762–1811)

Theodore Ledyard Cuyler (1822–1909)

Jonathan Edwards (1703–1758)

Andrew Fuller (1754–1815)

James Gilmour (1843–1891)

Alexander Viets Griswold (1766–1843)

T. D. Harford-Battersby (1822–1883)

David Livingstone (1813–1873)

Alexander Maclaren (1826–1910)

Robert Murray M'Cheyne (1813–1843)

Charles McIlvaine (1799–1873)

Aimee Semple McPherson (1890–1944)

F. B. Meyer (1847–1929)

D. L. Moody (1837–1899)

Handley Moule (1841–1920)

George Müller (1805–1898)

Andrew Murray (1828–1917)

John Newton (1725–1807)

Phoebe Palmer (1807–1874)

Joseph Parker (1830–1902)

William Swan Plumer (1802–1880)

William Henry Ridley (1816–1882)

Hester Ann Roe Rogers (1756–1794)

Charles Simeon (1759–1836) and
Benjamin Jenks (1646–1724)

A. B. Simpson (1843–1919)

Sadhu Sundar Singh (1889–1929)

Charles Spurgeon (1834–1892)

Susannah Spurgeon (1832–1903)

Maria W. Stewart (1803–1879)

C. T. Studd (1860–1931)

T. De Witt Talmage (1832–1902)

Henry Thornton (1760–1815)

Lucy Thurston (1795–1876)

R. A. Torrey (1856–1928)

Sojourner Truth (1797–1883)

Stephen Tyng (1800–1885)

Henry Venn (1724–1797)

Charles Wesley (1707–1788)

John Wesley (1703–1791)

B. F. Westcott (1825–1901)

George Whitefield (1714–1770)

William Wilberforce (1759–1833)

George Williams (1821–1905)

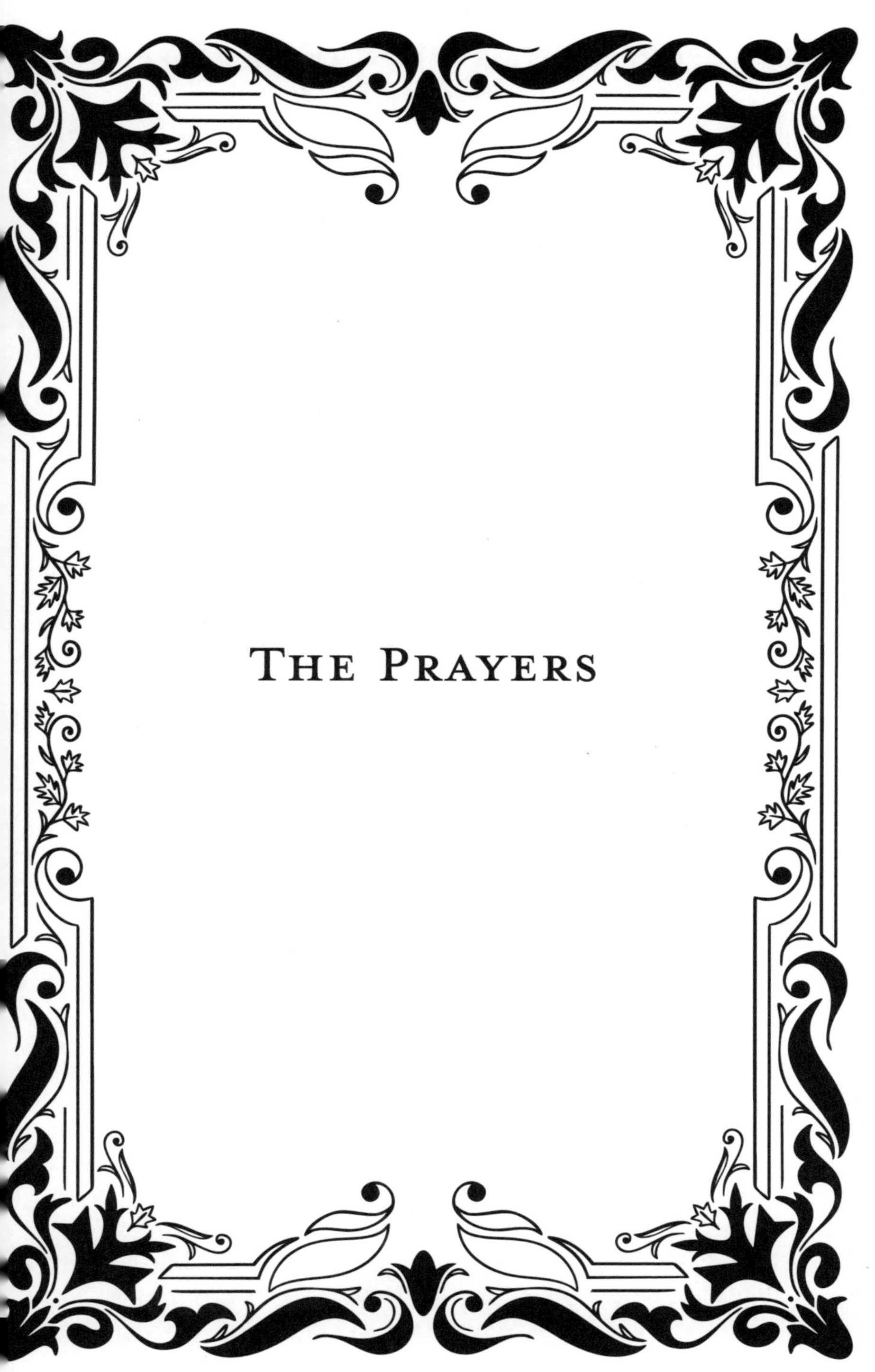

The Prayers

We Commit Ourselves to Your Service

Here is my covenant today

Eternal and ever-blessed God! In deepest humility I desire to draw nearer to you, in the name and for the sake of Jesus Christ. l present myself before you, though I fully recognize my infinite unworthiness to appear before you, to enter into covenant with you.

Even though my sins have made such a separation between you and my soul, I beg you, through Christ your Son, to grant me your presence. Accept the best sacrifice I can make.

I solemnly make an entire and perpetual surrender of all that I am and have unto you. In your strength I renounce all former lords who have had dominion over me. I turn away from every lust of the eye, flesh, and mind. I want to live entirely devoted to you and to your service.

I consecrate to you the powers of my mind—whatever you have given me or will give me. Help me to learn and prepare for any sphere of life where you will place me.

I dedicate all my possessions, my time, and my influence—all to be used for your glory.

I resign all I have to you and your direction, trusting the future into your hands. In all things may your will be done, not mine. Use me, O Lord, as an instrument of your services.

I beg you: Number me among your people! Clothe me with the righteousness of your Son forever. Impart to me, through him, all that I need of your purifying and cheering Spirit!

Enable me to live according to this my vow, constantly avoiding all sin. And in that solemn, awful hour when I come to die, help me to remember this covenant. Would you also remember it, Lord, and admit my departing spirit into your realm!

And when I am laid in the dust, if any surviving friend should encounter this memorial, may it be a means of good. Would you allow that one to have a part of your grace covenant, through Jesus the great mediator. To you and to the Father and your Holy Spirit be everlasting praises, lifted up by saints and angels. Amen!

—Jonathan Edwards

I OFFER MYSELF TO YOU

Dear Master, your blessings and gifts have filled my heart to overflowing with gratitude and praise. But the praise of heart and tongue are not enough until I prove by my deeds that my life is devoted to serving you.

Unworthy though I am, I thank you and praise you for bringing me out of death into life. You have made me to rejoice in your fellowship and love.

I do not know myself or what I need. But you know your creatures and their necessities full well. I cannot even love myself as you love me. To love myself truly is to love with heart and soul that boundless love which gave me being, and the love that you are.

So you have given me but one heart, that it might be fixed on one only: on you, who created it.

Master, to be seated at your feet is far better than to sit upon the highest throne of earth, for it means to be enthroned forever in the eternal kingdom. And now, on the altar of these sacred feet, I offer myself as a burnt sacrifice. Accept me in your grace. Wherever and however you choose, use me for your service. For you are mine, and I belong to you. You took this handful of dust and made me in your own image. You granted me the right to become your child.

All honor and glory and praise and thanksgiving be unto you forever and ever, amen.

—Sadhu Sundar Singh

I WANT TO BE RECREATED IN YOUR IMAGE

My God, let the idea of you as my Creator come to me not just in words, but in power.

May I experience that subordinate and complete submission I owe to the mighty sovereign who made me, and who is all in all.

And may your Spirit, who caused this world of beauty and order to emerge from chaos, operate with the same result on my dark, murky, ruined soul. I pray for the light that shines in the heart. May your Spirit awaken me, and may Christ give me light.

Do not let me forget the likeness in which I was created, nor the promised restoration of what has been lost. As I look to the one who made the worlds, O God, may I be transformed into his image. May I strive to recover the image of God, and to be perfect even as my Father in heaven is perfect.

All things were very good as they came out of your hand, Lord. You made humans upright, but they sought their own ways. Corruption springs from the creatures; they are led away by their own lusts. So let me look outward from myself, upward to the only source of every good and perfect gift.

You have never changed. We want to look to him who is the brightness of your glory, your image incarnate, so we may be transformed into your own image by studying and imitating the character of Jesus Christ.

He is the same today, yesterday, and forever. Amen.

—Thomas Chalmers

You will be our judge

O Lord God Almighty, we are not our own. Our hands, feet, head, heart, soul, mind, strength, time, and body ... all belong to you. You are our maker, and you will be our judge.

Though we have sinned, do take us just as we are. Make us yours by divine grace. Grant that we may obtain mercy from you in that great day, when you will judge the secrets of all by Jesus Christ. In that day, may we be found in Christ, and our names appear in his book of life.

Adopt us as your children. Let us never go astray from you. Teach us to keep your word and find delight in serving you. Apply to us the precious blood of Christ, and be our God, and Father, and friend forever.

We do not ask to be great, or rich, or to have the praise of others. But we do ask that our poor sinful souls may be saved.

We ask all for the sake of Jesus Christ. Amen.

—William Swan Plumer

Absolute surrender: I am yours

On the table of my heart rests a covenant, dear Lord. It is one I would like to renew with you, and to which I pray you would set your seal and signature:

I am yours, and all that I have.

Let my soul hear your tender response: I have called you by your name. You are mine.

You know there is nothing on earth I desire so much as to be absolutely surrendered to you, and to your service. I want the fullest spiritual blessing you see fit to give me. To obtain this, I gladly yield up body, soul, and spirit—all that I am and have—into your loving hands. Reign over and rule within me as my absolute king and master.

Have I counted the cost? Yes, Lord. And it means "I have been crucified with Christ. It is no longer I who live, but Christ who lives in me. And the life I now live in the flesh I live by faith in the Son of God, who loved me and gave himself for me" (Galatians 2:20).

This is the cost, but your grace is sufficient to meet it, and to fill your child's heart with joy unspeakable at the thought that I am no longer my own, but bought with a price.

Who has so great a right to me as you? Created by you, I belong to him who made me. Daily preserved by you, the life you maintain ought to be consecrated to your service. But the closest tie of all is that you have loved me, redeemed me from death, bought me with the price of your own blood, and so bound me to yourself forever.

Grant that my surrender may be real, practical, and complete—not in word only, but in deed and in truth. Not simply a spiritual submission, but a constant denial of self.

My time must not be aimlessly frittered away for self-indulgence, but every hour should bear on its fast-flying wings the witness of something said, or done, or thought, for you. My money all belongs to you, and every coin of it should be spent with your approval. So it is no longer a question of surrender, but only of quiet, happy submission as your will unfolds each day and directs my work and my way.

Lord, keep me ever thus in the secret hiding-place of your love, "as having nothing, yet possessing everything" (2 Corinthians 6:10). This is so safe a shelter for a weary, waiting soul, and so blessed a way of being made ready for the coming inheritance. Amen.

—Susannah Spurgeon

Here is my dedication covenant

From here on, O Lord, I covenant afresh and dedicate all my power to serving you. I give myself into your hands once more, as clay in the hands of the potter, in order that your whole will and pleasure may be accomplished in me.

My Savior and Redeemer, will you accept this offering? Allow me to me feel from this moment that you do. Let my plea be answered. Show us your power to transform and save to the uttermost, though trials of inconceivable magnitude may await me. I rely on your faithfulness.

If only I had the power to not live one more moment to myself. May my all—consecrated to you from this moment on—always glorify you in every way.

In the past I was ungrateful and did not serve you with my whole heart. Enough of that! I praise you now for allowing me to bear your holy cross. In your grace, I choose it now as my source of greatest glory.

Strengthen me, Lord. I am weak, but you are everlasting strength. You are my portion.

You have promised that I will not be tempted beyond what I can bear. But if you see at any time that my faith is about to fail, remove the trial, or cut short the work in righteousness, and take me home to yourself. Do not allow me to live to dishonor you.

Amen.

—Phoebe Palmer

Let us know what it means to be your children

Our God and Father, we ask that by the power of the Holy Spirit you would help us to enter into the responsibility of being your children. Of being "born of God" (1 John 5:4).

Father God, we your children know a little of it, and we can speak about it a little. We can enjoy it in some small measure. That we are your children, that we are "of God."

But all this is still just a little.

We know little of the power of being "of God," of being your children. So we pray and beg you, by the power of the Holy Spirit, write this so deeply on our hearts. Impress it so deeply, and so deeply affect our hearts by the consideration of being "of God," of being your children, that from now on it will be uppermost in our hearts—until our last moment on earth.

We ask it for Christ's sake, amen.

—*George Müller*

You pierce my ear

My possessor and sovereign, I will not go out free. You have pierced my ear at your door already and forever. But let it be done again, now and for the little lifetime of this new day which I open with this morning before you.

For its whole course, hour and minute, morning, noon, and night, I declare myself your personal property. It is all yours: my time, my position and reputation, my resources, my tongue, my imagination, my will. Even my spirit, soul, and body.

I surrender myself to you, not in dreamland or poetry, but in the commonplaces of today.

You know my path, my cares and joys, my tasks and opportunities. You know my home, my circle, my profession, business, handicraft, household service, my mission, my calling.

And in these things, as long as they are your will for me, I do yield myself to you. I am yours in this secret hour. Amen.

—Handley Moule

Let me be a servant

My Lord, I give myself to you to live this blessed life of service.

I have seen it in you. The spirit of a servant is a kingly spirit, from heaven and lifting up to heaven—the Spirit of God's own Son.

Everlasting love, dwell in me, and my life will be like yours. The language of my life to others will be like yours: "I am among you as the one who serves" (Luke 22:27).

Glorified Son of God, you know how little of your Spirit dwells in us, how this life of a servant is opposed to all that the world sees as honorable or proper. But you have come to teach us new lessons of what is right. You have come to show us what is thought in heaven of the glory of being the least, and of the blessedness of serving.

You, who not only gives new thoughts but implants new feelings, give me a heart like yours. A heart full of the Holy Spirit. A heart that can love as you do.

Lord, your Holy Spirit dwells in me. Your fullness is my inheritance. In the joy of the Holy Spirit I can be as you are.

I yield myself to a life of service like yours. Let the same mind be in me that was also in you, when you emptied yourself by taking the form of a servant. Yes, Lord. As a child of God let me be the servant of others. Amen.

—*Andrew Murray*

I WILL TO SERVE YOU

Now I come, Lord. I come.

I have put away my idols. I have put away everything that stood between me and you. I will to serve you. I will to follow you. I will to put my neck under your yoke forever, asking no more questions.

I am willing for you to lead me wherever you will.

Now, Lord, I come—you receive. Amen.

—Catherine Booth

Mold me like clay, Lord

I am your servant, Lord! I await your guiding hand to feel, to hear, and to keep your every word. To prove, and to do your perfect will. With joy I cease from all my own works, glad to fulfill all your righteousness.

If you condescend to use me, the humblest of your creatures, you choose the what, the when, and the how. Let all my fruit be found of you. Let all my works be done in you, and may you bring them to full perfection.

May you overrule my best, though weak, efforts. Change them as you see fit. Jesus, let all the work be yours. Your work, O Lord, is all-complete, and pleasing in your Father's sight. You alone have done all things right.

Here I leave all that is yours—to you. Mold me as you would passive clay. But let me always receive your stamp. Let me obey all your words. Let me serve you with a single vision.

And may I live and die to your glory. Amen.

—John Wesley

Set us free to serve

Set us free, O Lord, from the shackles of sin and earth, that we may joyfully serve you and labor on at your command.

O Lord! Truly I am your servant. You have loosed my bonds. You set us free so that in your service we may find liberty. You honor us by letting us do your will.

When we wait before you, you incline our hearts to the joy of obedience and the blessedness of action for you. You draw us by mighty motives, and you inspire us with power that is not our own.

We are enriched by so many gifts from your hand, and enabled by so many inspirations of your grace. So grant that we may joyously wait upon you in all holy obedience.

And as the eyes of the servants are toward their master, so may ours be to you, our God.

Amen.

—Alexander Maclaren

Teach me how to serve you

Heart-searching God and Father, you have a right to me, as my creator and preserver, and because you have given your Son to be my Savior.

I thank you that eternal life has been offered to me through his atoning death. Thank you that the Holy Spirit has drawn my heart to you, and that you have called me to serve you.

May the Lord Jesus Christ dwell in my heart by his Spirit, and purify me and fill me unto all the fullness of God!

Lord, unto you I consecrate my heart, my body, my time, my possessions, my influence—all that I am and all that I hope to have in this world or another.

Teach me how to serve you, and may I never grow weary in doing your holy will. Let your word abide in me in all wisdom. And may your grace ever be enough for me.

Make me steadfast in faith, perfect in love, and abundant in labor. And when this poor heart stops beating here on earth, grant me admission as a sinner saved by grace into the higher, holier service of your heavenly kingdom, for Jesus's sake. Amen.

—Theodore Ledyard Cuyler

Change Our Hearts

Shape my desires

Lord, I offer you the desires which are shaped in me by the grace of Jesus Christ. Unite those desires to the desires of your Son, I pray. Regard them as his. He is pleading for me. And grant me what I so desire, for his sake, for your own glory, and my salvation, amen.

—John Wesley

Give me a humble heart

My God, you are good. You are wise. You are powerful. Be praised forever!

Give me grace to love and obey you.

I thank you, my God, for making and redeeming me.
I thank you for giving me food and clothes, and for promising to give me your love forever.

Forgive me all my sins, and give me your good Spirit. Let me believe in you with all my heart and love you with all my strength.

Let me be always looking to Jesus Christ, who is pleading for me at your right hand. Give me grace not to do my own will, but yours. Make me content with everything. The least of all the good things you give me is far more than I deserve.

Give me a lowly heart, Lord. Never let me think myself better than anyone else, but as the very worst of all. And let me hate all praise, because you alone, O my God, are worthy to be praised. Amen.

—*John Wesley*

To the Eternal One from his tiny creature

O Lord, we want to honor you in humility and gratitude. In humility, because of the multitude of your mercies. And in gratitude, because we are unworthy of the least of them.

We are like feeble insects; you are the Ancient of Days. You have no end, and you are wrapped up in the still more awesome mystery of having never had a beginning. So the little circle we move in is a tiny spot in your immense works.

Your presence fills all space, and extends through the immeasurable fields of creation.

All the power of our thought and attention are taken up with petty personal interests, or with humble family concerns. But your all-seeing mind is everywhere. You preside in high authority over every world. At a single glance you take in the endless variety of life. Yet even the tiniest of your works does not escape your notice.

But blessed be your name, you permit us to approach you! We are your creatures, and we have the privilege of your mercy. Your all-seeing eye never abandons us. You have given us a part in this wider scene of glory.

You have taught us to confide in your goodness. Though we are feeble and sinful, we rejoice in the hand that formed us, guides us, and sustains us.

Yet how miserably little gratitude and obedience we show you! Our ways are corrupt. We are children of guilt and disobedience. Our best attempts to love and serve you are random and feeble.

Look with pity on our weakness and errors, Lord. Fill our hearts with a serious, permanent habit of faith. May it be something more than just a momentary impulse, more than a feeling that is excited by an eloquent sermon or enthusiastic prayer. More than an emotion we may feel when cares or distractions seem far away, or which fill our hearts during a communion service or a quiet Sunday evening—when peace is all around.

Establish your empire in our hearts, Lord. May it reign supreme over our thoughts, purposes, and affections. And may it be with us in solitude as well as in public, at work as well as in the house of prayer.

May it be our life's goal to live out a grace-filled picture of Christian faith to the world, to let the world see the difference that Jesus can bring. Amen.

—Thomas Chalmers

Remind us that we are your children

O Lord, help us to ponder it a thousand times more than as yet we have pondered it: That you have regenerated us, made us a new creation in Christ, and made us your very own children. Not merely calling us, but making us. That you give us spiritual life, heavenly life.

This is the wondrous grace we should ponder. This is the "kind of love the Father has given to us" (1 John 3:1).

O Lord, help us by the power of your Holy Spirit to lay it to heart a thousand times more than as yet we have laid it to heart. And grant that, by considering it, praying over it, and laying it far more abundantly to heart, our hearts may be filled with love toward you. Make us then grateful, more than ever.

Grant it for Jesus Christ's sake, we pray, amen.

—George Müller

Pour into me your fountain of love

You are love, blessed Father. And only those who abide in love abide in you and in fellowship with you. Today the blessed Son has again taught me how deeply true this is of my fellowship with you in prayer.

O my God! Let your love, poured out in my heart by the Holy Spirit, be in me a fountain of love to all those around me. May the power of believing prayer spring out of a life in love.

O my Father! Grant by the Holy Spirit that this may be my experience—that a life in love to all around me would be the gate to a life in the love of my God. Help me to find in the joy with which I daily forgive whoever might offend me the proof that your forgiveness to me is power and life.

Lord Jesus, my blessed teacher! Teach me to forgive and to love. Let the power of your blood make the pardon of my sins such a reality, that the forgiveness you show me and the forgiveness I show others may be the very joy of heaven.

And show me anything in my dealings with others that might hinder my fellowship with God. That way, my daily life in my own home and in society may be the school in which strength and confidence are gathered for the prayer of faith. Amen.

—Andrew Murray

Help me to know the power of the cross

Precious Savior, I humbly ask you to show me the hidden glory of the fellowship of your cross.

The cross was my place, the place of death and curse. You became like us, and have been crucified with us.

Now the cross is *your* place, the place of blessing and life. And you call me to become like you, and as one who is crucified with you, to experience how entirely the cross has made me free from sin.

Lord, help me to know its full power. It is long since I knew the power of the cross to redeem from the curse. How long I struggled in vain as a redeemed one to overcome the power of sin, and to obey the Father as you have done!

I could not break the power of sin. But now I see: this comes only when your disciple yields entirely to be led by your Holy Spirit into the fellowship of your cross. There you make me see how the cross has broken forever the power of sin and has made me free. There you, the Crucified One, live in me. There you impart to me your own Spirit of whole-hearted self-sacrifice to cast out and conquer sin.

Oh my Lord, teach me to understand this better. In this faith I say, "I have been crucified with Christ" (Galatians 2:20).

You who loves me to the death, I seek you—the Crucified One. Not your cross, but you. I hope in you. Take me, Crucified One, and hold me tight. Teach me moment by moment to see that everything from self is condemned—worthy only to be crucified.

Take me and hold me. Teach me, moment by moment, that in you I have all I need for a life of holiness and blessing. Amen.

—*Andrew Murray*

Make us shine like you

Let us draw near to you. May we go forth to abide in you.

Give us your light and life, and then we cannot help but shine, because we will be just like you. And in your overflowing life we will be a blessing to others, even more than the blessing we receive.

Come to us now and light up the sanctuary of our heart. Reveal to us the heavenly bread until we eat and are satisfied.

For your own dear name's sake, amen.

—A. B. Simpson

I WANT THE DIGNITY OF LOVE

Oh, precious Savior! Save us from maligning your gospel and your name by clothing it with our paltry notions of earthly dignity, and forgetting the dignity which crowned your sacred brow as hung upon the cross!

That is the dignity for us, and it will never suffer by anyone carrying the gospel into the back slums or alleys.

That dignity will never suffer by any employer talking lovingly to his worker, and looking into his eyes with tears of sympathy and love, and trying to bring his soul to Jesus.

That dignity will never suffer even though you should have to be dragged through the streets with a howling mob at your heels, like Jesus Christ, if you have gone into those streets for the souls of your fellow humans and the glory of God.

Though you should be tied to a stake, as were the martyrs of old, and surrounded by laughing and taunting fiends and their howling followers—that will be a dignity crowned in heaven, crowned with everlasting glory.

If I understand it, that is the dignity of the gospel—the dignity of love. I do not envy, I do not covet any other. I desire no other—God is my witness—than the dignity of love. Amen.

—Catherine Booth

Help me to deny myself

Lord, I confess that I have dared to set up my will against yours. I have acted as if I were independent of you. Though I profess Christ, I have not been ready to deny myself and take up my cross. I have cherished and indulged the cravings of my corrupt nature. I have encouraged those sinful affections of my heart which I should have strangled at birth. I have even thought that happiness in life consists of fulfilling the lusts of the flesh and the mind.

I have sinned against you, God. Not just in open rebellion, but in the general direction and business of my life. My carnal mind has been set against you. I have resisted your authority.

Show me my guilt, Lord, until holy shame overwhelms and I return to you. And give me your Holy Spirit, so that through him I may put to death all the deeds and lusts of this body.

May my table never become a snare, and may my plenty never lead to excess in eating or drinking. Help me not to pamper my body or walk in lust. Fill me with constant dread not just of sexual sin, but of every expression of impurity of the eye, tongue, or heart. Give me an aversion to foolish talk, filthy jokes, and to all entertainment that defiles the mind and wars against the soul.

Give me the urgency, day by day, to cry to you: Keep me blameless in spirit, soul, and body! And may I never gratify any appetite you have given me, other than in the way you intend.

Enable me to vanquish my natural desire for riches or worldly greatness. Make me content with what I have, never coveting. Give me power to resist any love of money, the root of all evil. And give me a suspicious eye for any complacency that comes with any prosperity you give. Keep me satisfied with yourself, Lord, as my all-sufficient portion!

Put to death the pride of my heart and whatever thirsts for approval or honor from others. Let my ambition be only to please you. Conquer my selfish dread of being resented or mistreated for the sake of righteousness. Make me always ready to confess my faith.

Cleanse me, O God, from out-of-proportion affection for created good and comfort. May even my nearest and dearest relations or friends never take a wrongful place on my heart's throne, in the place reserved for God himself.

God be merciful to me, a sinner, through the atonement and for the sake of him who was delivered for my offenses and raised again for my justification. Amen.

—Henry Venn

A prayer in prosperity

Blessed God, you are rich in goodness and mercy. You are my inheritance and my cup. I am surrounded on every side with your mercies. I give you glory, Lord. You have dealt so well with your unworthy servant and provided me with such great and so many blessings.

But I do not know what will happen tomorrow, or how soon the sun that now shines on me will be hidden. Grant, Heavenly Father, that this world may not be my portion. May I not abuse the world's good to your dishonor and my own undoing. May I never turn your generous gifts into weapons of rebellion against you. Enable me to use them in proper fear of you, and to serve you even better in proportion to the obligations you lay upon me.

Make me also willing to refresh my poorer brothers and sisters. Help me to give to them as freely as I myself have received. As I have opportunity, let me do good to all—especially to those who are of the household of faith.

Gracious Lord, preserve me from the danger and destruction that so often comes with prosperity. I would rather you deprive me of all my earthly possessions than allow them to impede my progress toward your heavenly kingdom.

Even if you should make me poor or give me trouble, let me be content and bless your name—as much when you take from me as when you give to me. And whatever I have here to enjoy, let me never set my heart upon it. May

I never trust in uncertain riches, but in the ever-living God.

Preserve me from pride and forgetfulness of you, from love of the world, and from all other vices or corruption that might come with riches. And let none of my abundance or success in the world ever puff me up with pride or conceit, or scornful disdain of others, or wanton rebellion against the Lord.

Do not let me turn from you, but draw me nearer to yourself with cords of love. Let me enjoy the fullness of your grace and be rich in faith and good works. And may my soul prosper and be made glad with your saving mercy and your acceptance of me in Jesus Christ. Amen.

—Charles Simeon and Benjamin Jenks

A PRAYER OF DEDICATION

What kind of a heart is mine that feels so little, loves so little, repents so little! Send me light, Lord, to show me my heart. Send me grace to change my heart. Cleanse it, humble it, refine it, strengthen it, and warm it.

I want to be crucified with Christ and live—not to myself or the world, but unto God. I want to live by faith in the Son of God, who loved me and gave himself for me (Galatians 2:20).

But why do I live so far from you, Lord? Why am I so ignorant of your unsearchable riches, so cold to your wonderful love, and so devoid of your heavenly mind? Why am I so dull and blind to the power of godliness? Why am I so selfish, lazy, proud, impatient, and unbelieving? Why is there so little meekness, gentleness, and self-denial in my life?

Why do I care so much about what others think of me, and so little for what you think? Why am I so unwilling to be despised, opposed, or rejected by others, when Jesus was so despised and rejected?

Why do I feel so much as if the world were my home, and realize so little of its futility and depravity? I pay so little attention to the claims of eternity or the attractions of heaven.

Why am I not burning with the love of Jesus and holy love for others? I fall far short in all things, and how little I regret it! Where is my panting after God, my hungering and thirsting after righteousness, my pressing toward the mark?

Sin killed me first. Now that by grace I have been revived to newness of life, sin still cripples my efforts. It clouds my views, clogs my affections, and contaminates all my attempts at serving God.

Where can I flee for hope? Left to myself I perish. Jesus, Lamb of God, I flee to you alone! In you is all. You call me to yourself; help me to come!

Teach me to sit at your feet and learn in your school. Show me how to lean on your grace, take up your cross, and rejoice in your promises. I bring my heart to be changed and set apart by your Spirit. Breathe into me the breath of life, that I may become a living soul!

As my life's single ambition, I want to focus on your glory. I want to concentrate my affections on serving you, and in you alone is the power to do so. Jesus, if you will, you can make me clean. Increase my faith. Appear in my heart, bless me, and revive me. Amen.

—Charles McIlvaine

Let me lay low

Lord, do I choose to be saved in the way which gives you all the praise, and me none?

And do I not only see it to be the Bible way of salvation, but does it resonate in my heart as delightful?

Search me and try me, Lord. I can only answer, "Yes, yes!"

Is it the desire of my heart to be made altogether holy? Is there any sin I want to keep? Is sin a grief to me, especially when it suddenly rises and overcomes?

Lord, you know all things. You know that I hate all sin, and want to be made altogether like you. And the sweetest words in the Bible are: "Sin will have no dominion over you" (Romans 6:14).

Oh, then, that I might lie low in the dust—the lower the better—so that Jesus's righteousness and Jesus's strength alone will be admired! Amen.

—Robert Murray M'Cheyne

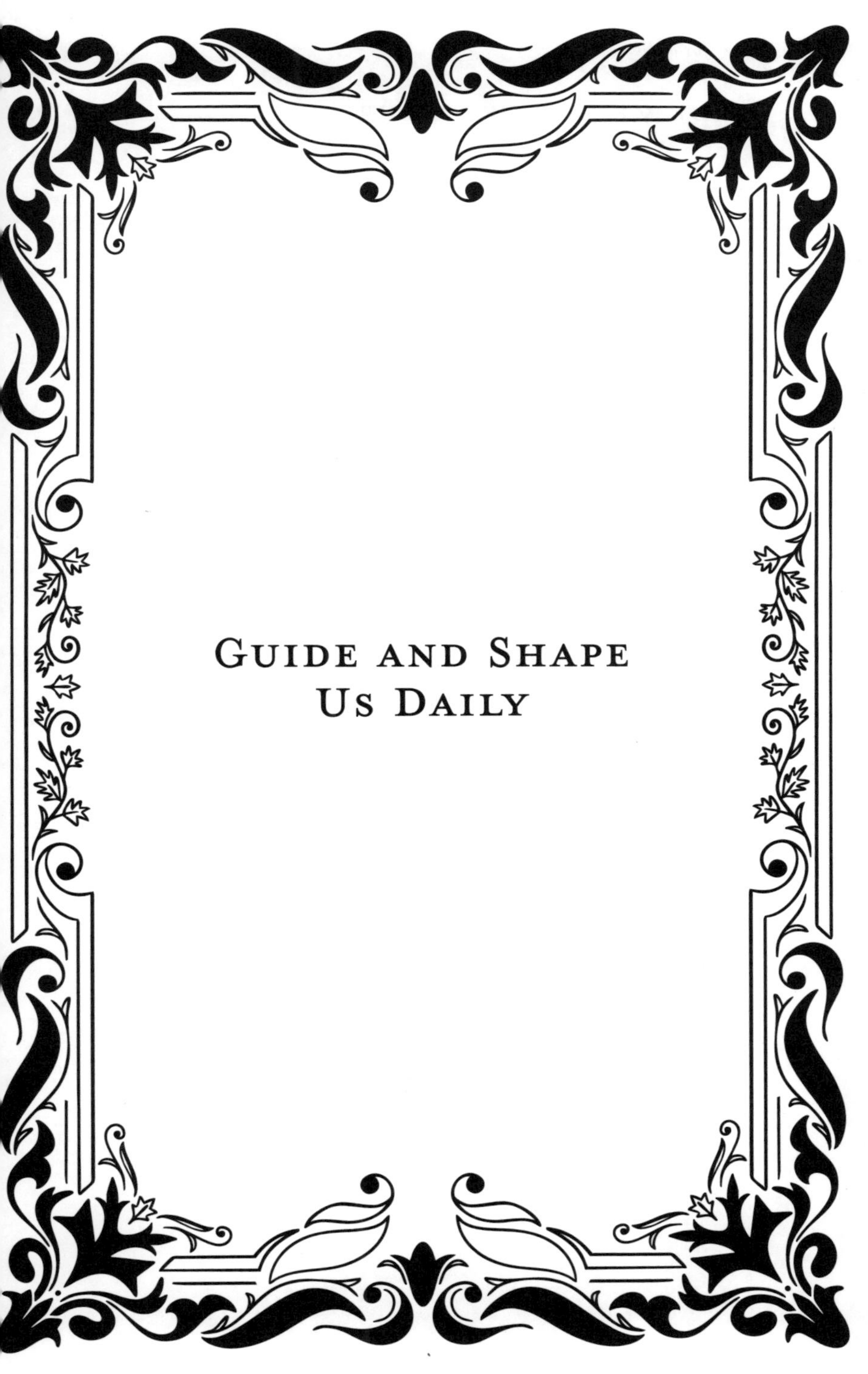

Guide and Shape Us Daily

Guide me out of failure

When I look back on my life and see how little I have done for you, Lord, I am ashamed and humbled in the dust. May I better employ any time that remains.

You know all my failings. Sadly. You know my errors, infirmities, and negligence. But you are all goodness and patience toward me.

Meanwhile I come to the cross with all my sins, negligence, and ignorance. I cast myself on the free mercy of God in Christ as my only hope and refuge. Lord, receive and pardon me. Give me your renewing grace.

Take charge of me, and tune my heart to sing your praises. Make me wholly yours.

Guide me, guard me, purify me, strengthen me. Keep me from falling, and ultimately present me faultless before the presence of your glory with exceeding joy. Amen.

—*William Wilberforce*

A plea for God's will and guidance

Oh Lord, you have brought me here and supported me up to this time, and you still do now. I ask your direction. Not for honor, wealth, or luxury, but only to glorify your name.

Now I cry to you; I plead in the name of Jesus: Lord, enable my ears to hear a word behind me saying "This is the way, walk in it." Oh my God, if it is not in your will, may something prevent it. But if it be in accordance with your mind, then bring it to pass. Enable me to feel I am in the path where you would have me to go.

Oh Lord! By your wisdom and strength all will become right, but help me to be more humble and patient. Guide my judgment and keep me in the right way. Amen.

—George Williams

May we live our lives like Jesus

Most holy and kind God, our Father in heaven, you have said, "Seek my face." Give us hearts to say, "We will seek your face, Lord."

We are blind, and we cannot see far. Teach us.

We are guilty. Forgive us.

We are unholy. Cleanse us.

We have served the wicked one. Bring us to serve you.

Help us to walk with you, God, and to draw our hopes and comforts from your holy word. Give us humble hearts.

Let us never tire nor grow weary in trying to please you. Let us love you above all things. Teach us how to put our trust in Christ alone. Do not give us up to our own vile hearts. Grant that our best days—and all our lives—may be given to you, God.

And when we die, may we die the death of the Righteous One, and our last end be like his.

We ask it all for Christ's sake. Amen.

—William Swan Plumer

Show me now your way

Lord, my position at this moment, in your presence, and at your feet, abundantly proves that I have already found grace in your sight. Otherwise you would not have called me by name, and taught me in that way to seek your favor.

And now that I am admitted to the audience-chamber, and you have graciously held out to me the golden scepter, help me, O Lord, to present my petition, that you may give me what I ask.

Show me now your way.

You know how blind I am by nature, how often I am puzzled and astonished by your dealings with me, and how often the way before me is dark, hidden, and rough. Throw a ray of heavenly light on all that seems indistinct and gloomy.

Let your way be lit up by the clear shining of your love. Then how easy and pleasant it will be to walk in it! In days gone by, I have sought and strived to go my own way. And Lord, it has been sorry traveling indeed. But now your grace has made me not only willing but determined that my feet will tread no other path than that which is set for me! Amen.

—Susannah Spurgeon

Turn my way into your way

"Make your way straight before me" (Psalm 5:8).

Dear Father, this cry is going up to you now from a tried and perplexed soul who is fearing to wander in the wilderness, where there is no way.

Will you graciously bend down your ear, listen to this prayer, and grant the direction and guidance?

Dear Lord, it is not that your ways are ever crooked, but that my eyes are bent on seeing pleasant little bypaths, where the road is not so rough or the walking so tough, as on the King's highway. My way looks so enticing, so easy, so agreeable to the flesh. Your way means self-denial, taking up the cross, and the denying of much that my heart desires. Are not these very things the guideposts which show me the right road?

Now, dear Lord, hear my cry, "Make your way straight before me." Compel me, by the power of your love and your example, to take the narrow road. Hedge up my way with thorns (Hosea 2:6) rather than that I should take a step out of your way you have laid down for me.

What if, sometimes, the fog is so thick that I cannot see the path? It is enough that you hold my hand and guide me in the darkness. Walking with you in the gloom is far sweeter and safer than walking alone in the sunlight.

Dear Lord, give me grace to trust you wholly, whatever happens. Help me to yield to your leading, and lean hard on you. Your way for me has been marked out from all eternity, and it leads directly to you and home. Help me to keep my eyes fixed on the joy set before me, and deliver me from the faintest desire to turn aside or linger in flowery meadows which have lured the feet of poor pilgrims into danger and distress.

Father, you have said, "My thoughts are not your thoughts, neither are your ways my ways" (Isaiah 55:8). And that is true. But you can lift my thoughts to yours, and raise my ways until they reach the mountaintop of obedience to your blessed will.

Work this miracle for me today, O Lord. Use that sweet compulsion which will delight my heart while it directs my steps. Make me run in the way of your commandments, and I will run gladly, with the blessed certainty that I will reach the goal at last.

Have you not given me a monitor within which strikes a gentle warning note when my feet turn even an instant from the straight way? But, best of all, dearest Lord, come with me yourself along life's road, today and every day! Let the abiding of my soul in you be so real and constant, so true and tender, that I may always be aware of your sweet presence, and never take a single step apart from your supporting and delivering hand! Amen.

—Susannah Spurgeon

You are my everything

My hope, my God and Savior—you are my light and way, my life and health, my glory and grace. Look down from your throne with favor on those for whom you endured so much.

You are the living and true God. My gentle and kind master. My great king. My good shepherd. My only teacher. My most ready helper. My true and living bread. My everlasting high priest. My guide to my own country. My reconciliation and peace. My sure defense. My most desirable portion. My unblemished sacrifice. My perfect redemption. My assured hope. My resurrection from the dead. And my everlasting life.

I pray that I may walk by you, come to you, and rest in you who is the way, the truth, and the life, without which no one comes to the Father. You are the blessing my soul desires, my only Lord.

I pray that you would not let me turn back. Instead help me to move forward in my affections until you at last bring my whole spirit, soul, and body into the peaceful mansions where my heart is already fixed.

I can already taste the firstfruits of the Spirit. Grant to me the entire gift, and fill my soul with the joys which I anticipate. Collect my scattered thoughts and remove the blemishes and deformities of my present frailties, until I resemble your beauty and you establish me forever in the glory of your blessed presence, O God of my salvation. Amen.

—*Stephen Tyng*

Give us clean hands and answer prayer

Heavenly Father, increase my faith today. Give me a strong faith in you and in your word. Help me to realize what I have read about you—that nothing is too hard for you. I know that you are able to reach unbelievers, scoffers, pantheists, and atheists. I know you can reach the abandoned and fallen and lift them up, and purify them in the precious blood of your Son.

I pray that you will do great things here in the coming days. May they be days of your power. I ask not for the power of man, but for the power of God. I pray that the Spirit of the living God may be here.

I pray that the fear of God may fall upon this place, and that waves of salvation would go out all over the land. May I not limit your power, O God, but expect great and mighty things.

Help me to turn away from every sin, so that I may lift up clean hands to you, and my heart may be pure in your sight, and so that you will answer my requests.

Let the Holy Spirit come down upon me and remain, and may my heart be on fire with holy fire, and Christ will have the praise and the glory, amen.

—D. L. Moody

When I don't know what to do

God of wisdom and might, you have graciously commanded your poor, short-sighted creatures to commit our works to you. You have promised to establish our plans (Proverbs 16:3). We are told to cast all our cares on you, with the assurance that you care for us (1 Peter 5:7). And in your mercy you hear.

But my mind is full of doubt and wavering about which course to take. My mind is fixed on you, my only counselor. Teach me what to do. Help me to choose the path that gives you the most glory and my good.

I know that you govern all things in heaven and earth, and you make all things work together for good to those who love you (Romans 8:28). Endow my soul with love for you, through knowing Jesus Christ, so that I may rest in you—and then wait without anxiety.

If things turn out in my favor, give me grace to credit your mercy entirely. Help me to remain always grateful. But if you think it best to hand me adversity, then grant me strength to behave well under your correction, and in my affliction to put my whole trust in your mercy. Help me to respond in submission and humility, in faith and patience. May the prosperity of my soul be promoted by the continuing weight of my troubles.

And may I be able to say in the end, "Faithful God, you have caused me to be afflicted. God of peace, patience, and consolation, your kingdom rules over all. Your dominion is from generation to generation, world without end, through Jesus Christ my redeemer, amen."

—Henry Venn

I want to work for you

Lord, what will you have me to do? Now I want to go to work.

—Sojourner Truth

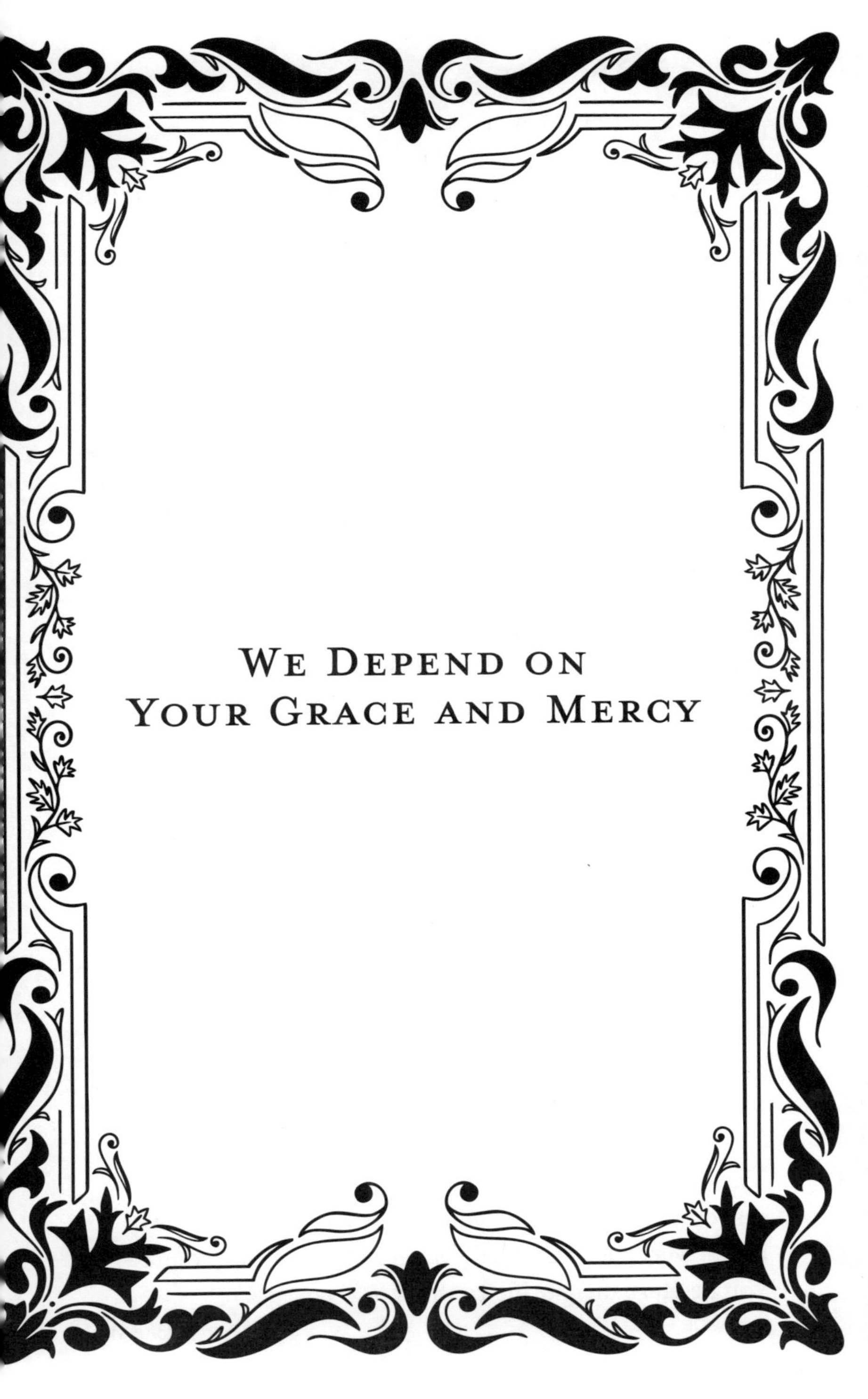

We Depend on Your Grace and Mercy

Water us with your grace

Lord, we are nothing before you—but you are everything to us.

We continue to be as nothing, after you have in double mercy drawn us out of nothing and out of sin. Of this we bear ceaseless proof in ourselves—in our continual weakness and helplessness.

We see ourselves in the midst of an ocean, for you are the true and boundless ocean of nature and grace. You spread abroad the waters of heaven in every age, as you please. You draw these waters back and send them again to the souls that you love.

But as we see how waters on the earth are corrupted and go stagnant if they cease to run, even for a little while, we have reason to fear. The same might happen to our souls if we hold back your heavenly waters instead of letting them return to you, their source.

Grant therefore, O God, that I may never take possession of your grace for only myself, any more than the air appropriates to itself the light of the sun. You withdraw it every day to restore it the next.

O give me the same ability of receiving and restoring your grace and your good works. I say *your.* For I freely admit that the root from which they spring is in you—and not in me.

The only grace we ask of you is that your grace may not rest on us, but return to you—and then descend to us again. May we be eternally watered by you, and so may you be eternally glorified. Amen.

—*John Wesley*

When I am spiritually sluggish

O Lord, I know not what I am, but I flee to you for refuge.

I surrender myself to you, trusting your precious promises, and against hope believing in hope. You are the same yesterday, today, and forever. So however cold and dull I am, yet, waiting on the Lord, I trust I will in time renew my strength.

Even now my heart seems to grow warmer! Oh let me fall again to prayer and praise, and earnestly request from you fresh supplies of strength and grace.

I have read too little of the Bible this week. Lord, give me spiritual understanding. Let me drink of the water of life. To you, O Lord, I fly for relief. Your promises are sure, and you will not turn away anyone who comes to you.

Here is what I rely upon: by commanding us to grow in grace, you show us that we may. Oh let me then rouse myself. Lord, enable me to purify myself as you are pure. Let me be deeply humbled at the footstool of your throne. I bow before you and plead the atoning blood of Christ, humbly trusting in his promises of pardon and of grace.

Lord, I cast my cares on you. I flee to you for relief. Savior of sinners, save me. Help, Lord! Watch over me, guide me, and guard me. Amen and amen.

—William Wilberforce

Help us to truly seek you, Lord

O Lord! Look upon the cold hearts which we bring to you now to be warmed and the feeble faith which we hope to have strengthened.

We come to you with confession as well as with thanksgiving. We have set up in our hearts many false images and have turned away from you far too often. But we pray for your pardoning mercy. And Lord, if we dare say it, we pray still more for your purifying grace, for your confirming steadfast spirit. Draw us higher and nearer to yourself.

We pray for guidance, for surely we are blind and dark. We pray for strength, for if we have any power it is too much for ill, and all the strength is yours both for doing and for willing that which is good.

Come to us, then, that we may do without fail those things that please you. Deliver us from all the oppression of our own faults and past evils. May they not have dominion over us.

Lead us into a large land of liberty and light and life. And may we walk before you there with glad hearts.

We praise you for your love, and thank you for the assurance of it—which we have. We bless you for him who is its seal and pledge, and its channel to us. And we ask that we may be more entirely and continually knit to Jesus Christ in faith, love, fellowship, and obedience, and so may be brought more fully into the fellowship of the Father and the Son.

Be near us, Lord, and receive us in grace. We will offer you our sacrifice of praise, through Jesus Christ our Lord and Savior, amen.

—Alexander Maclaren

I TRUST YOU BUT NOT ME

Every good and perfect gift comes from you, Lord. I look up to you for the grace and strength to do what you require. All my sufficiency is of you.

Lord, your footsteps are in deep waters. All things seem dark around me, even as you reveal your way of providence and grace. Will I ever see light and deliverance? "Light dawns in the darkness for the upright" (Psalm 112:4).

May I be found in that number!

Lord, I trust your promises, but I distrust myself. May it be my chief concern to seek first the kingdom of God and his righteousness, both for myself and my children. Then I can safely trust that every other needful good will be added. Amen.

—Andrew Fuller

I'M COMING SAFELY HOME

Blessed Master, the more I know of you, the more grace I find in your sight. And when you see anything of your own likeness in me, you will perfect and complete it.

You will draw me, and I will run after you. And the very fact of following you will clear my vision and enlighten my understanding, so that I may see and comprehend more of your beauty and precious worth—more of your marvelous grace to me.

You know that everything of earth tends to hide my Lord from me. Satan envelops me in dark clouds of unbelief. My own sinful heart blinds me. Cares oppress and crush me. Worldly fears gather around, intent on my bewilderment.

But, loving Savior, if I have found grace in your sight, nothing can separate me from you. You have taken me by the hand. And through all dangers, over all difficulties, and in spite of all enemies, you will lead and guide me safely home to yourself.

If I have found grace in your sight, show me now your way, that I may know you. Amen.

—Susannah Spurgeon

Fill our outstretched hands with mercy

O blessed Lord, your patience with us in the past has been a miracle of mercy! You have seen so much in us which your soul has detested, yet you come now with the gift of healing in your hands. That means not only pardon but the power to be holy.

Yet our own ways have led us farther and farther from you. So now let your forgiving, healing love draw us so close to you, that we can never again be among those "who forsake the paths of uprightness to walk in the ways of darkness" (Proverbs 2:13).

We lift up empty beggar's hands to your full ones. Place in our hands, we pray, all of your promised blessing that we can handle!

Amen.

—*Susannah Spurgeon*

Depending on the Holy Spirit

O Holy Spirit, love of God, powerful advocate and heavenly comforter, pour out your grace on me. Descend into my heart. Light the dark corners of this neglected dwelling, and scatter there your cheerful beams.

Dwell in my soul; it longs to be your temple. Water this barren soil, which is overrun with weeds and briars. It is lost for lack of cultivating. Make it fruitful with your dew from heaven. Heal the lurking distemper of my inward being.

Strike me through with the dart of your love, and kindle your holy fire in me. Make it flame in a bright and devout zeal. Burn up the impurity of sensual affections. And as you spread through every part of me, may you possess, purify, and warm my whole spirit, soul, and body.

Let me drink deeply of your spiritual goodness. And let its heavenly sweetness so correct my palate that it leaves no desire for unhealthy worldly delights.

Teach me to do what pleases you, for you are my God. Holy Spirit, I believe that in whoever you dwell, the Father and Son do likewise come. And happy is the heart which is honored with so glorious a guest! May it please you to come to me, comforter of mourning souls. You are a mighty defense to those in distress. You are always ready to help in time of need.

Come, strength of the feeble—the one who raises those that fall. Come, you who brings down the proud and teaches the meek and humble. Come, hope of the poor, who refreshes the weak. Come, guiding star for those who sail in this stormy sea of life.

Come, Holy Spirit, in your great mercy. Enable me to receive you. Bend down to me in my infirmities, that your strength may be made perfect in my weakness. Bring me to the feet of my Savior Jesus Christ, my only hope. In unity with you, Holy Spirit, he lives and reigns with the Father, one God, world without end, amen.

—*Stephen Tyng*

Help in my weakness

My heavenly Father, I have no strength in myself, but there is almighty power with you. Your heart is full of love toward me. And you have proved your wondrous love toward me by bringing me to Jesus, and by giving Jesus for me—a poor, miserable, guilty sinner.

Now help me in this my spiritual conflict. Let me not be overpowered by the subtlety of the devil, or on account of my spiritual weakness.

Help me! Help me! Help me! I know you are willing to help. Amen.

—George Müller

Deliver Us from Evil

Keep my conscience working

The heart is the worst of all.

Lord, do not let my conscience fade, the way it has before. You have convicted me of the spiritual danger I am in. Now work that conviction deeply into my heart, so that it produces a settled humility and an unceasing watchfulness against temptation.

And then ground that conviction with an awareness of how helpless I am, as well as how prone I am to offend you.

Amen!

—*William Wilberforce*

Our courage is from you alone

Just like us, blessed Lord, you were tempted in all things. Have mercy on our frailty. Give us strength from weakness. Help us to know that good, holy fear as we worship you and you alone. Come alongside us when we are tempted. Make us bold in dangerous times. Give us courage to do your work, and to keep on as your faithful soldiers and servants until the end of our days. Amen.

—*B. F. Westcott*

Save us from hypocrisy

Lord save us from hypocrisy and sham.

Shrivel the falsehood from us if we say we love you but do not obey you!

Are we staying at home and praying for missions when you have told us to go? Are we holding back something of which you have said, "Loose it, and let it go"?

Lord, are we utterly through and through true? Lord God of truthfulness, save us from sham! Make us perfectly true! Amen.

—Amy Carmichael

A prayer for protection

Almighty God, it is the glorious hope of a blessed immortality beyond the grave that supports your children through this valley of tears. I bless your name forever because you have implanted this hope in me.

If you have indeed plucked my soul from the fire, it is not because you have seen any worth in me. It is because of your distinguishing mercy, for mercy is your beloved quality. You delight in mercy, and are not willing that any should perish, but that all should come to know the truth in Jesus.

Clothe my soul with humility like a garment. Grant that I may bring forth the fruits of a meek and quiet spirit. Enable me to adorn the truths of God my savior by what I say and do. May I become holy and pure, even as you are holy and pure.

Bless all my friends and reward those who have given me a cup of cold water in your name. Forgive all my enemies. May I love those who hate me, and pray for those who despitefully use and persecute me.

Protect me from the malicious tongues of others, O God. Do not let my good be described as evil. And help me never to murmur or complain, but cheerfully bear with all the trials of life.

Clothe me with the pure robes of Christ's righteousness, so when he comes in flaming fire to judge the world I may appear before him with joy, not grief.

I ask these blessings not only for myself, but for all the sons and daughters of Adam. For you are impartial, and all distinctions wither in the grave. Grant that all prejudices and animosities may cease from among us. May we all realize that success comes not from the east or the west, but that it is God who lifts up one and sets down another.

May the rich be rich in faith and good works toward our Lord Jesus Christ, and may the poor have an inheritance among the saints in light, an incorruptible crown that never fades, eternal in the heavens.

And now what are we waiting for? Grant that we may at last join with all your people to celebrate your praise. Amen.

—*Maria W. Stewart*

May I be watching and waiting for you

Cleanse me, O God, from secret faults. Father, strip this poor unworthy worm of yours of every impure and unholy desire—from all self-righteousness, pride, hypocrisy, slander, and deceit.

Do you not have a blessing for me? Bless me, even me, my Father! Bless me when I go out and when I come in, when I lie down and when I rise up. Support me with your everlasting arms, and keep me from all evil.

I would sooner you extinguish my lamp of life than leave me to dishonor your cause or wound the hearts of your children.

Hold me in your hand or I will fall. Save me, Lord, or I perish. My mind is filled with gloomy doubts and fears. At times I fear to die, and death is the king of terrors. My Savior, take from me this awful fear.

And when I come to the bed of sickness, show yourself to me. Let me lean my head on you, and let guardian angels keep watch over my pillow. When pain and anguish fall on me, may I calmly say, "Did Jesus suffer this way, and now I should complain? O death, where is your sting? O grave, where is your victory?"

May this poor unworthy worm of yours be clothed with the breastplate of righteousness, and protected with the helmet of salvation. May the testimony of Jesus be within me, his seal engraved upon my forehead, and my name written in the Lamb's book of life. May I overcome the temptations of the wicked one and wash my robes white in the blood of the Lamb.

Present me faultless before the Father's throne, without spot or wrinkle or any such thing. And when you call me to go, may I not desire to stay, but rather to depart and dwell with you, which is far better. Amen.

—Maria W. Stewart

A PRAYER FOR A SINCERE CHURCH

Do not leave us, Lord. Deliver us from the temptations which surround us: seeking the praise of others, looking to others, ignoring the wounds of your people.

People say of us, no doubt, that we meet to please ourselves with pleasant singing, with nice sermons and such, and that we go away just as we were before, only better pleased with ourselves. Deliver us, good Lord, from this great snare. Let the work be deep and real. Let there be a thorough cleansing of the temple in every corner—removing all the filth and corruption that has been allowed to accumulate.

Let there be a full coming up into the light, and then help us to abide there. Amen.

—T. D. Harford-Battersby

Keep me from wandering

O Lord, open my eyes to see the danger I am in—the evil of my nature and life.

Open my lips to confess my wickedness. Open my heart to receive your word, so that I may join in the praises your people pay you. Do not let me perish (as I would without your mercy) clutching a lie.

Time is short, death is near, and it may be sudden. Lord, enable me to consider the things belonging to your peace—before they are hidden from my eyes!

Now, Lord, I am yours. I vow to follow you, for you have redeemed me.

Should I continue in sin because grace has abounded? God forbid! I am crucified with Christ, crucified to the world, and the world to me. The love of Christ now compels me. The time past is sufficient to have lived in vanity. From now on I am the Lord's. You have bound me by tender mercies to present myself, body and soul, to your service. Here, O Lord, I offer my whole self, all that I am, and all that I have, a living sacrifice, holy and acceptable to you.

O let me never, never wander from you again, but let me walk in the light, as you are in the light. Let me have communion with you here below, until you remove me out of the reach of sin and sorrow forever. Amen.

—*John Newton*

Help! My mind wanders ...

I wander more than ever, Lord, and I can scarcely keep awake. My thoughts are always straying. O God, set my affections on purer pleasures. Christ should be my delight and glory.

With your help I will focus and long for the joys of heaven, for deliverance from this world of ingratitude and sin. Keep me from impatience and spiritual fatigue as I anticipate the crown of victory.

If I live daily under the impression of your presence, God, yet I do not always keep true to you. Every night I look back on a misspent day—or at least one not improved with fervent faith and diligence. O God! Enable me to live more to you, to focus on Jesus, and gradually see the renewed nature implanted in me. Let me see this heart of stone removed.

But I see plainly the sad path I am on. The sense of your presence seldom stays with me, and at times I even have doubts and difficulties with the truth of the great doctrines of Christianity.

Of myself I have not power to change. O Savior of sinners, have mercy on me. Let me not be one who despises your goodness and patience, inviting wrath.

Because with God, nothing is impossible. Amen!

—William Wilberforce

Give me victory over Satan

My God, give me the victory. And let the wisdom—and meekness of wisdom—which you alone can inspire, carry me in safety through this terrible warfare to a haven of peace.

O may your word, and the providences that surround me, serve as effective instruments in the hands of your Spirit to repel the assaults and ploys of our cruel and skillful enemy.

"Resist the devil, and he will flee from you" (James 4:7). "Take up the whole armor of God" (Ephesians 6:13). "Do not be anxious about anything, but in everything by prayer and supplication with thanksgiving let your requests be made known to God" (Philippians 4:6).

Satan is now bruising my heel. May the captain of my salvation bruise his head and fulfill the promise that Satan will soon be bruised under my feet. Keep me focused on that end, but not with constant vain and restless brooding about things that annoy me or that I do wrong. Instead, keep me striving toward godliness.

And let the law of the spirit of life in Christ Jesus free me once and for all and forever from the law of sin and of death. Amen.

—Thomas Chalmers

We Cling to You in Tears and Trouble

When I am persecuted for believing

God forbid I should love father, mother, brothers, or sisters more than you, blessed Lord. No! I have long since given you my soul and my body. I now freely give you also my friends.

I find that things today are just as they once were. Those born of the flesh persecute those born of the Spirit. You came not to bring peace, but a sword. And unless we leave behind everything, we cannot be your disciples.

So I come to do this part of your will, my God: I am assured that "everyone who has left houses or brothers or sisters or father or mother or wife or children or lands, for my name's sake, will receive a hundredfold and will inherit eternal life" (Matthew 19:29).

Lord, I trust it is for your sake alone that I now offer you the favor of my friends. Enable me to plug my ears to false insinuations. They favor things of this world, not things of God. And without your help they would cause me to deny the Lord who bought me.

I should not be surprised at this kind of offense, Lord. It comes to try what is in my heart. So I bless your holy name that I am counted worthy to suffer for you. Let me rejoice and be very glad that my reward will be great in heaven. Take me into your arms of mercy. From here on, whoever does the will of my heavenly Father—they will be my brother, and sister, and mother.

Lord, I know this will expose me to the derision and persecution of those around me. But you sought out and revealed yourself to the poor beggar who was cast out by the Jewish council. Reveal yourself also to me, when my friends and the world call me evil. Enable me to pray for them—even when they persecute me. Forgive them, for they don't know what they do.

It is only because of your free mercy that I have come to know you and the power of your resurrection. Let the same grace be enough for them also. Make your mighty power known to them for their conversion, as well.

You magnified your goodness once by turning your servant Paul from a bitter persecutor to a zealous preacher of the gospel. And you made the trembling jailer cry out, "Sirs, what must I do to be saved?" So I beg you—look down in compassion on my family. Use me or someone else to strengthen my weak brothers and sisters. Even though we are now divided, may we in the end glorify you with one heart and one voice.

Amen and amen.

—George Whitefield

We accept the good— and the not-so-good

Lover of souls, should we not be simply, heartily, and wholly yours?

Should we refuse the cup of affliction from your hand? Or should we drink the cup of sinful pleasure, when we remember what our sins have cost you?

Should we want to be loved by the world that despised you? Should we be ashamed to profess our attachment to such a savior?

No, Lord. Forbid it! Let your love compel us. Let your name be glorified, and your will be done by us and in us. Let us count all things loss and dung for the excellence of knowing Christ Jesus our Lord.

Let us not desire anything you see fit to withhold, nor yearn to part with whatever you call for.

Let us always prefer your love above even the greatest temporary, worldly joys. Amen!

—John Newton

Prepare me for battle in this culture

Lord, I feel like one who is about to launch into a stormy sea, and who knows from fatal experience how little my own powers are equal to its strength.

O Lord, equip me for it. Enable me to seek your glory, and not my own. Let me keep watch in prayer and wait diligently on you.

Help me to love you my redeemer from the heart, and to be held tightly by this love to live actively and faithfully. Help me to devote all my faculties and powers to serve you and those around me.

Especially let me work faithfully and humbly the tasks you set before me, as unto the Lord, and not people. Help me to submit patiently to your will.

And if it is your will that we should be defeated in our effort to deliver our country from the load of guilt and shame which now hangs round her neck, like a gangrene eating out its vital strength, gradually preparing for its ruin?

Then O Lord, lead and guide me. Amen.

—*William Wilberforce*

Would you dry every tear?

O Lamb of God, your ear is ever open to our cry. Tender, loving Jesus, whose heart is ever yearning over your little ones, fix every eye upon yourself today.

As the moon and the stars withdraw their shining before the sun at noonday, let earthly cares and hindrances pale and disappear before the glory of your power and presence. Stretch out your arms, our Father, and enfold this suffering multitude unto yourself.

Dry every tear, banish every pain, relieve the oppressed, heal the sick, and forgive the sinner every sin. Draw us up close, Son of God. As a father pities his children, so you pity those who love and trust you.

Give light in place of darkness. Give hope in place of fear. Give comfort and sweet confidence to each heart gathered in your presence, for your own name's sake. Amen.

—Aimee Semple McPherson

Talk to Us Through the Storm

Blessed Christ who came to the cities around Lake Galilee, come in mercy to all our great cities of today!

You who put your hand on the foaming billows of the lake and made them lie down at your feet, hush all the raging passions of the world!

On the night when the disciples were trying to cross this lake and the wind was against them, and after nine hours of rowing they had made only three miles, you came stepping on water.

As you said to the drenched disciples, would you now say to all your people, in whatever kind of storm they are in: "Take heart; it is I. Do not be afraid" (Matthew 14:27). Amen.

—T. De Witt Talmage

I will praise you in trouble

Gracious Father, I cannot pray for you to spare me from trouble. Send just what you think is best for me. Only ... when you do, be always close to comfort and strengthen me. Work all things for good. That way, I can praise you for my afflictions in the end. Amen.

—William Henry Ridley

We look to you in our tears

Blessed be your dear name, O Lord, for your strong consolation and "good hope through grace" (2 Thessalonians 2:16).

Tears may, and must, come. But if they gather in eyes that are constantly looking up to you and heaven, they will glisten with the brightness of coming glory. Amen.

—Susannah Spurgeon

A NEW WAY TO LOOK AT WORRY

"Let not your hearts be troubled" (John 14:1).

Dear Lord, these words of yours, though so sweet, are a command to be instantly obeyed. Perhaps I have never before looked at them in this light, never realized that in carrying within me a troubled spirit, I am acting in direct disobedience to you.

Say the words over again to me, dear Lord! And with your gracious command, issue also the mighty power which will enable me to fulfill it. How often must I have grieved you by my lack of trust in your tender love and care! How often you must have marveled at my foolishness in trying to bear burdens which might have been cast at your feet.

Let not your heart be troubled. Truly, I hear a serious note of rebuke and disappointment mingling with the music of these sweet words. It may be so, dear Master, for after all that you have done and said, my heart should never be troubled. I should not let it be afraid.

And yet how soon does fear overtake the steps of joyful assurance? How quickly do I pass out of the light of your presence into the deep shadow cast by the mountain of my sin?

Lord, help me to reason with myself about this. Or rather, say to me, "Come now, let us reason together" (Isaiah 1:18). For then I know that your infinite love will silence my fears and hush all the anxiety of my soul. Amen.

—*Susannah Spurgeon*

You take me from briers to myrtles

Blessed Lord, how tender and merciful you are to me. Yet this is your sweet way toward all who trust you.

"Instead of the thorn shall come up the cypress; instead of the brier shall come up the myrtle; and it shall make a name for the LORD" (Isaiah 55:13).

When depression and sadness come to me, when the thorns and briers of daily cares and vexations prick and tear at me, then you turn my footsteps to where the pines and myrtles of your loving mercies grow. In their shelter and fragrance my troubled spirit finds rest.

Even more, your power is so great that you sometimes transform the very things that hurt and grieved me into means of grace and blessing to my heart and life. Disappointments and obstacles in my work, the estrangement of friends, incompetence and weakness, or an overpowering sense of deepening responsibility ... these experiences are all like thorns and briers, which irritate and worry.

Yet they vanish when you give the word, and I wonder as I find myself walking peacefully among the fir trees. Pine needles spread the softest of carpets under my tired feet. And the myrtle's snowy blossoms promise perfume and sweetness even to those who bruise them.

Your ways, O Lord, are past finding out, but they are very gracious and tender. And this turning of seeming evil into good, of making your children's trials grow into triumphs, and their pains into pleasures, is a wonderful proof both of your pity and your power.

"It shall make a name for the LORD." My Father, can this be really so? Does your great name receive added glory when you prove your sovereignty on my behalf? When I come to the next sharp thorn-hedge in my path, will it honor you if, instead of trying to force my way through it (and getting wounded for my pains), or trying to avoid it by some roundabout way (and plunging deeper into the thicket), I should just calmly sit down before it, and pray, and wait for you to wither it up or turn it into a myrtle grove?

Yes, and I seek faith and grace from you to do constantly this otherwise impossible thing. Dear Lord, when troubles come, I want to learn to look upon them as ways and means of glorifying you. I want to accept them as tests and trials of my faith, and to meet them with a brave heart, expecting the salvation of God! If my pathway were always smooth and pleasant, with never a thorn or brier to trouble me, there would be no opportunity for the glorious exercise of your love and mercy in deliverance from them.

Give me grace to say with Paul, "I will boast all the more gladly of my weaknesses, so that the power of Christ may rest upon me" (2 Corinthians 12:9). Amen.

—*Susannah Spurgeon*

When things are going badly

Most holy and righteous God, you order all things in heaven and earth. With the greatest tenderness you hear the cries of all who put their trust in you, through Jesus Christ.

I believe (Lord, help my unbelief) that in wisdom, mercy, and holiness you appoint every circumstance of my condition. I want to look through all second causes to you, Lord. You make them merely instruments to do your will and execute your purpose.

Infinitely wise and gracious governor of the world, I have often said "Your will be done." But now that you choose to afflict me, I am ready to shrink back, to be demanding or fretful under the sacred but painful cross. What I have often so solemnly repeated, I am strongly tempted to unsay, and to wish for my own will, not yours.

Hurry, God of my salvation; help me to deny myself. Fill my soul with perfect submission. Convince me that you, and you alone, know what kind of correction I need. You see the foolish perversity and sinful disorders of my soul; you alone can adapt a remedy to the disease.

In the midst of my troubles, Lord, let your comforts refresh my heart. Relieve the weariness and pain by the supernatural support of your grace. I know however dark this night of affliction seems, if you say, "Let there be light," there will be light. Let me patiently wait and quietly hope until that time of mercy comes.

And as my foolish heart is ready to grow fond of this earth, let the disappointments and afflictions I meet here loosen my affections and put an end to all my sinful attachments to any thing below. Through Jesus Christ, amen.

—*Henry Venn*

Help us in our daily work

Lord, enable and fit us for our daily tasks, whatever they may be. May we carry your name into them all.

And when the heavy assignments come, or perplexing circumstances, or sore temptations, or gnawing anxieties, with sorrows that weigh us down, Lord be close. Shape in us your grace which is more than enough for our deepest needs.

We pray, Lord, that you would help us understand where our true comfort and strength are. And if in anything we need consolation, keep us from seeking it in the wrong places. Help us to turn to the Father of mercies, the God of all comfort whose consolations are neither few nor small.

Help us to be your faithful, humble, loving, lowly servants and soldiers until our life's end. Amen.

—*Alexander Maclaren*

Amid daily troubles

We put our life into your hands, Lord. It was yours before it was ours. It will be yours again. We brought nothing into this world, and it is certain we can carry nothing out. Our days are swifter than a flying shadow, and none remain forever. Help us while it is called today to call upon you with our whole heart and to serve you with our whole strength.

We have come to bless you for blessings at home: for the care of the little ones, for the light that has made our house glad, for all the successes this week. Hear us when we praise you for your grace—for your close and tender presence amid distraction, darkness, and trouble upon trouble.

Help us always to bear the burden and to walk steadily across the swamp. Enable us to find the bridge that you have built over every difficult river. And help us to see the meaning of it all, giving praise to him who by many a hidden way has led us to the common rest.

Keep our hearts and minds in the love of Christ. Save us from becoming bitter. Spare us from the distress of wrath, discontent, and lack of love. Help us to forgive our enemies as we ourselves are forgiven by God. May we live the noble life and breathe an ever-enlarging prayer as we realize the ever-gracious blessing of our Father's presence. Amen.

—Joseph Parker

We Seek Your Presence

I TRUST YOUR PROMISE OF YOUR PRESENCE

O Jesus, you have said, "I will come to you" (John 14:18).

You have said, "I will send [the Helper] to you" (John 16:7).

You have said, "My Father and I will come unto you, and make our abode with you" (John 14:23).

You are God who cannot lie. I wholly rely upon your most true promise. Accomplish it in your time and in your way. Amen.

—Charles Wesley

We cry out for you

O Lord, whether we know it or not (and we often do not know it), our heart and our flesh cry out for the living God.

We ask that we may turn these cries into prayers, and that they may be the prayers of faith that are seconded and backed up by our daily lives. That way, we may receive your blessings. Lacking them, we would continue always to be miserable and poor and blind and naked, and all the while fooling ourselves to have need of nothing.

Show us our great wants, Lord, and then give us your great gifts. Fill us with the power and the peace of your own life bestowed through Jesus Christ, who is our life.

And help us, day by day, to live the lives that we live by faith of the Son of God, who loved us and gave himself for us. Amen.

—Alexander Maclaren

You see us! Draw us closer

O Lord, who dwells in inaccessible light, we thank you that we can draw near and walk in the light by him who is the light. And we come to you now, though our eyes are feeble and your light is full of glory.

We draw near as your children. We want to come close to your heart. Even though you are far beyond all thought and blessing hearts can touch. You let us love you and nestle close.

We pray then, O Lord, that you would do more than just permit us to come to you. We ask you to draw us to yourself. For surely you know the way to the hearts and minds you have made.

Bring us near to yourself. And help us so that, day by day, amidst all our changing circumstances, perplexities, and duties, we may still be able to keep our communion with you, and to walk in your presence rejoicing to think that you, God, see us.

Amen.

—Alexander Maclaren

Where are you, God?

As a night without stars, so is my soul, O Lord, if you hide your face from me! My feet falter, my steps are uncertain, my hands grope as at midnight. My heart is oppressed by an unspeakable fear and dread.

O blessed light of my life, what has caused you to withdraw yourself? Why are you hidden behind thick clouds, so that I cannot rejoice in you?

Sadly there can be but one answer to the question, and it is a very serious and sorrowful one: "Your iniquities have made a separation between you and your God, and your sins have hidden his face from you" (Isaiah 59:2).

O my Lord, this indictment is all too true, but I have acknowledged my transgressions: "I despise myself, and repent in dust and ashes" (Job 42:6).

I hate the sin that so constantly surges up within me, defiles my holiest service, and dares intrude even into my prayers. You know my cry goes daily, almost hourly, up to you: "Heal me, O Lord, for my bones are troubled. My soul is also greatly troubled. But you, O Lord—how long? Turn, O Lord, deliver my life; save me for the sake of your steadfast love" (Psalm 6:2–4).

Amen.

—Susannah Spurgeon

Reveal yourself to my heart

My gracious God, when you show me your way, you draw me closer. You touch my eyes, that I may see. You reveal yourself to my heart, so I can understand your will.

You allow endearing communion with you which overwhelms my soul—a foretaste of heaven.

There were times when you were a stranger to me, when I did not recognize your love or take seriously your claims. But now with divine power you have shown yourself as the Lord and master of my spirit. And with intense desire I long to know you and the power of your resurrection!

And there is nothing my heart craves more passionately than "the light of the knowledge of the glory of God in the face of Jesus Christ" (2 Corinthians 4:6).

I understand your amazing love and grace ... somewhat. But to be able to plunge into the great deeps of your covenant mercies, to soar into the limitless space of your faithfulness, to travel from east to west of your pardoning love, and never find a boundary to your sympathy and power—this would be to taste of the unspeakable joy which glorified spirits know.

Dear Lord, if I have found grace in your sight, will you not at least so sweetly reveal yourself to my waiting heart? Then I would be compelled and enabled to exclaim, "This is my beloved and this is my friend" (Song of Solomon 5:16). Amen.

—*Susannah Spurgeon*

Help me to know the mystery of your love

You showed them your hands and feet.

Blessed Master, that must have been the most marvelous sight that men or angels ever looked upon! The creator of all worlds standing as a sacrifice for sin before his own fallen creatures!

God in the flesh, laying bare the wounds which atoned for their transgressions!

It passes comprehension.

Lord, enlighten my understanding, so I may know something of this mighty mystery of incarnate love! Amen.

—*Susannah Spurgeon*

Show me your glory!

Show me your glory, God! I feel deeply how utterly impossible it is to lift myself up or make myself live for your glory alone, by any effort of my own.

But if you will reveal your glory to me—

If you make all your goodness pass before me and show me how glorious you are—

If you show me how there is no glory but yours—

If you let your glory shine into my heart and take possession of my inmost being—

If, my Father! Then I will never be able to do anything but glorify you. Then I will only live to make known what a glorious, holy God you are.

Lord Jesus, you came to earth to glorify the Father in our sight. You ascended to heaven, leaving us to do it now in your name and in your place. Give us by your Holy Spirit a vision of how you did it. Teach us the meaning of your obedience to the Father—your declaration that his will must be done at any cost.

Teach us to heed your confession of the Father, how you testified what he was to you and how you felt about him. May we with our lips also proclaim what we taste of the Father's love, so that others may glorify him.

And above all, teach us that redeeming love has its triumph and joy in saving sinners. Show us that God has his highest glory in holiness, casting out sin.

And take possession of our whole heart so we may love and labor, live and die, for this one thing: that "every tongue confess that Jesus Christ is Lord, to the glory of God the Father" (Philippians 2:11).

O my Father, let the whole earth, let my heart, be filled with your glory. Amen.

—*Andrew Murray*

I NEED TO KNOW YOU!

O my God! How can I thank you for this wonderful grace? Your Son became man to teach us the blessedness of a life of human dependence on the Father. He lived through the Father.

We see in him how the divine life can live, work, and conquer here on earth. And now he is ascended into heaven, and has all power to let that life work in us. We are called to live even as he did on earth. We live through him.

We praise your name, God, for this unspeakable grace.

And now hear the prayer I offer: If it may be, show me more—much more—of Christ's life through the Father. I need to know it, my God, if I am to live as he did.

Oh, give me the spirit of wisdom in the knowledge of him. Then I will know what to expect from him, what I can do through him. It will then no longer be a struggle and an effort to live according to your will and his example. Because then I will know that his blessed life on earth is now mine, according to the word: As I live because of the Father, so you will also live because of me (John 6:57).

Then I will daily feed upon Christ in the joyful experience. I live through him.

Father, grant this in full measure for his name's sake. Amen.

—Andrew Murray

Everything else is not enough

You, O Lord my God, are above all things best. You alone are most sufficient and most full. You alone are most sweet and all comfort.

You alone are most fair and most loving. You alone are most noble and glorious above all things. You are the one in whom all things are at once and perfectly good, and ever have been and will be.

Therefore whatever you bestow on me beside yourself, or whatever you reveal or promise about yourself—so long as I do not see or fully enjoy you—is too little. It fails to satisfy me.

And that is because my heart cannot truly rest or be entirely content unless it rests in you. Unless it rises above all your gifts, above all created things.

When will I fully become aware of who I am in you, that through the love of you I may not feel myself but you alone—above all feeling and measure? Amen.

—*Amy Carmichael*

A PRAYER FOR REFORMATION

O Lord my God, inspire my soul with a holy desire for you—to seek you and to find happiness in finding you. Help me to express that love by turning from all my past wickedness.

You are my king. Subdue and expel my rebellious passions. Reign absolute in my heart and kindle in it the bright fire of your love.

You are my redeemer. Drive out the spirit of pride and replace it with your own humility.

You are my savior. Take away my anger and give me instead the shield of patience.

You are my creator. Root out my bitterness or resentment and implant in me gentleness of temper.

You are my most merciful Father. Grant your own child the best gifts: a firm and right faith, a steadfast and well-grounded hope, and a never-failing love.

O my director and governor, take away all vanity and filthiness of mind, a wandering heart, a vulgar or abusive tongue, or a proud look. Preserve me from the venom of slander and detraction; from the itch of curiosity; from the thirst of covetousness, ambition, and vanity; from the deceit of hypocrisy; from the secret poison of flattery; from contempt of the poor or oppression of the helpless; from the canker of envy and the fever of greed; and from the pestilence of blasphemy and profaneness.

Purge me of injustice, rashness, and stubbornness; from impatience, blindness of heart, or cruelty. Incline me instead to obey what is good and to follow wholesome advice. To bridle my tongue and restrain my hands from wrong. Do not let me insult the poor, defame the innocent, or despise those less fortunate. And help me to show affection, kindness, and compassion to those around me.

Fountain of mercy, show me how to practice love and mercy. Teach me tenderness toward those who are afflicted. Show me how to do what I can to relieve misery, supply needs, and comfort sorrows.

May I have a heart to help the oppressed, aid the injured, sustain the needy, and cherish the dejected. May I also release those who owe me, pardon whoever offend me, and love those that hate me. Help me to return good for evil and despise none, but pay all due respect to everyone.

Set a watch before my mouth, and keep the door of my lips. Wean my affections from things below, and let me be eager and fixed upon heaven and heavenly things. Amen.

—Stephen Tyng

We need you now, Jesus!

O Christ of God! Compassionate man of Calvary.
All-powerful, almighty King of heaven and earth.
The sun who dispels all darkness.

Lion of Judah, who breaks every chain. Deliverer of the captive. Hope of the hopeless, and friend of the friendless. Son of the Living God.

If ever we loved you, or needed you, or trusted you—
it is now.

Weak, helpless, desperate, we hide, hide away in you.

O rise up! Rise up, dear Son of righteousness, with healing in your wings. Lay bare your mighty arms, and glorify your name. Amen!

—Aimee Semple McPherson

Wake Us and Revive Us

Mold me into your image

Almighty and everlasting Father, accept my humble sacrifice of praise and thanksgiving. Thank you for calling me out of darkness into your marvelous light, for bringing me to life when I was dead in sin.

You have told us that your Holy Spirit should be in us, a well of water springing up unto eternal life. Finish, then, the good work begun in my soul. Now that you have called me, never let me lie down again in sin.

You see the good seed sown in my heart. As yet it is a very small grain of mustard seed. With the dew of your heavenly blessing, continue to water what your own hand has planted—and it will become a great tree.

You have touched the eye of my mind by your divine power. Let your Holy Spirit remove what scales remain, more and more, until I eventually see all things clearly.

With shame I confess I am unworthy of this and all your other mercies. I had crucified the Son of God and put him to open shame. But you are rich in mercy to all who call upon you. In faithfulness forgive me what is past, and grant from here on that I may work out my salvation with fear and trembling.

I know that as you begin to deliver me from bondage, I must expect to pass through a barren and dry wilderness. I know there are lions in my way before I reach a true soul Sabbath. But preserve me from the snares and fury of those who would overtake and destroy my soul.

Make me teachable like a little child. Grant that I may be willing to learn what things I ought to do, and grant me the strength to do them. Strengthen me, I beg you, by the Holy Spirit. Help me to lay aside every weight, especially the sin that so easily besets me. Help me forsake all and even lay aside my own life to be your disciple.

Do not allow me to deceive my own soul by a partial reformation. Search me and try me, and examine my heart, and let no secret lust or passion ever keep me from everlasting life.

Lord, I am not my own. You have bought me with the price of your Son's most precious blood. See! I now give you my heart, without keeping back the smallest part. For who do I have in heaven but you? What could I ever want here on earth that would compare to you?

Mold me into your own blessed image, my Lord and my God. Fill me with your grace here, and fit me for your glory hereafter. Amen and amen.

—George Whitefield

Rouse me fully, sanctify me completely

O Lord, quicken me. Bring me alive! I am a sluggish believer. But blessed be God, it need not always be so. You have declared that you will be found by those who seek you.

I fly to you, O Lord. Forgive and receive your unworthy wanderer.

Come and dwell within me! How forgetful am I of the presence of God. O Lord, fill me with love, brotherly kindness, and grateful humility.

How thankful should I be for my unique privileges, and how shocking to think that I have been seeking God for years, yet I have grown so little. O Lord, I would humbly hope that though I am weak and feeble, yet Christ is knocking at the door of my lukewarm heart, and that I will now open the door and admit my heavenly visitor.

O Lord, rouse me fully. Make me an active, zealous, fruitful Christian. Oh most blessed promise, that you will freely give the water of life to whoever is thirsty! So as the main spring has been set flowing, may it water every distant branch.

Oh how little have I done to honor you, and how much better do people think of me than they would if they knew me as I really am!

Lord, sanctify me completely. Amen.

—*William Wilberforce*

Come revive us, Lord

Oh Lord, revive your work in my heart.

The world with its influence has had much claim upon me, and Satan has taken the advantage. While the body has been busy Satan has suggested ease and indulgence, which (sadly!) I have given way to.
Do not be angry forever, Lord. Come again and revive your work, that your dust may be useful and desire to glorify you and feel the power of your Holy Spirit.

The deep spirit of prayer and devotion seems to have faded. Oh Lord, come again, come now and revive true devotion in our hearts. Pour upon us the power of the spirit of prayer. How many there are among us moral characters, almost converted, yet yielding to the world!

And now, oh Lord, I pray that you would give me from this hour a double portion of your Spirit so that I may do your work, and so that very many souls may be converted and saved. Amen.

—*George Williams*

Bring me to life

O my Lord, my religion, my faith, my love, my enthusiasm—all die out so soon. My warmth disappears and is in danger of departing altogether!

Stir up your grace in my heart, I pray. Fan the flame of love and zeal within me. Lift me up out of the dust. Make me diligent and lively in faith. Set me forward once again, that I may strive more and pray more, and may know and feel more of your help and presence. Then I can rejoice more in you.

I am very dull, slow to give thanks, and discouraged when you do not stir me up.

Revive me, I pray, as you see best, amen.

—*William Henry Ridley*

I don't want to settle for less

Ah, Lord! Your poor child sorrowfully confesses to falling very far short of the high standard of Christian life to which your word expects.

Along with so many others, my life just seems to be winding down—when instead I might have life, and have it more abundantly (John 10:10).

I know that the possibilities of being conformed to Christ are only to be measured by the exceeding riches of your grace and greatness of your power. Yet I sometimes seem content without full participation in the glorious experience your love offers.

Lord, enlighten and quicken me, I pray. Put forth in me the mighty grace which will make my daily life a proof that you are working your own will in me. Help me to know, at least in some measure, "what is the immeasurable greatness of his power toward us who believe" (Ephesians 1:19). Amen.

—Susannah Spurgeon

Revive this church!

Lord, raise up in our churches many men and women that are all on fire with love for Christ and his gospel. Give us back again men like Antipas, your faithful martyr. Men like Paul, your dedicated servant who proclaimed your truth so boldly. Give us Johns, men to whom the Spirit may speak, who will bid us hear what the Spirit says unto the churches.

Lord revive us! Revive your work in all the churches. Return to the church of God in this country. Your enemies think they have it all their own way, but they will not, for the Lord lives, and blessed be our Rock.

Roll up your sleeves and show us your strength in these last days. Shepherd of Israel, deal a heavy blow to the wolves and keep your sheep in their own true pastures, free from the poisonous pastures of error.

We know you do not sleep, yet sometimes it seems as if you do sleep awhile and leave things to go on in their own way. We beg you: Wake up! And we know your answer: "Awake, awake, put on your strength, O Zion" (Isaiah 52:1). We would do this, Lord, but we cannot do it unless you put forth your strength to turn our weakness into might.

Great God, save this nation! O God of heaven and earth, stay the floods of infidelity and filthiness that roll over this land. People seem entirely indifferent. They will not come to hear the word as they once did. God of our fathers, let your Spirit work again among the masses. Turn the hearts of the people to hear the word, and convert them when they hear it. May it be preached with the Holy Spirit sent down from heaven.

Our hearts are weary for you, the king who is forgotten in your own land. The king who is despised among your own people. When will you again be glorious before the eyes of all? Come, we beg you, come quickly. Or send forth the Holy Spirit with a greater power than ever, so our hearts may leap within us as they see miracles of mercy repeated in our midst.

Father, glorify your Son. Bless all work done for you, whether in the barn or the cathedral or in the Sunday school. Let the holy service of prayer never cease, and let the intercession be accepted by God, for Jesus Christ's sake. Amen.

—Charles Spurgeon

Cure our sleeping sickness

Good Lord! Baptize us with the Holy Spirit and with fire.

Cure us of all this dread plague of sleeping sickness, this crazy talking in our sleep, even as we unceasingly pray, "Your name may be hallowed everywhere, your kingdom come speedily, your will be done on earth as it is in heaven."

Amen and amen!

—C. T. Studd

May we live while we live

Lord, we want to live while we live. We pray that we may not merely groan out an existence here below, nor live as earthworms crawling back into our holes and dragging now and then a dry leaf with us. But help us to live as we ought to live, with new life that you have put into us, and that lifts us up.

Do not let us always be hampered like half-hatched birds within the egg. May we chip the shell today and get out into the glorious liberty of the children of God.

Lord, visit our church. We have heard your message to the churches at Ephesus; it is a message to us also. Do not let any of us lose our first love. Do not let our church grow cold and dead.

We are not, we fear, what we once were. Lord, revive us! All our help must come from you. Give back to the church our love, our confidence, our holy daring, our dedication, our generosity, our holiness. Give back all we ever had and much more. Take every member and tenderly wash our feet, sweet Lord. Set us with clean feet in a clean road, with a clean heart to guide us.

Bless us, our Father, and let all the churches of Jesus Christ enjoy the same care and tenderness. Make our lights shine. And now unto Father, Son, and Holy Spirit be glory forever and ever. Amen.

—*Charles Spurgeon*

Set Our Hearts on Things Above

Make me a faithful steward, and make me content

Sovereign and all-bountiful God, you make us poor and you make us rich. You govern all things in heaven and earth. Accept my sacrifice of praise and thanks for giving me all things richly to enjoy.

What am I, O Lord, or what is in me, that I should have bread enough and to spare, while so many are ready to perish with hunger? It is not my merit, but your mercy. Not my foresight, but your sovereign good will.

But do not let my prosperity destroy me! As you have made me rich in this world's goods, make me rich toward you—rich in faith and good works. Do not let me say to gold, "You are my hope and confidence."

Do not let me trust in uncertain riches, but in you, the everlasting God. Don't let me lay up for myself treasures on earth, where moth and rust destroy, and where thieves break in and steal. Grant that I may lay up treasures in heaven.

Lord, I know this is humanly impossible, and that it is easier for a camel to go through the eye of a needle than for a rich person to enter the kingdom of heaven. But Abba, Father, all things are possible with you. In your grace, enable me to deny myself, take up my cross, and follow you every day. Give me that faith which overcomes the world. Grant that I might not indulge myself in the lust of the eye or the pride of life. Instead, help me be hospitable. Help me to visit your people when they are ill or in prison. Help me to take in strangers, to clothe, feed, and give them something to drink.

May I be eyes to the blind, feet to the lame, and a parent to the orphan. May I encourage the widow. Help me to follow you, Jesus. Though you were rich, for our sake you became poor. You came not to be served but to serve. Help me to remember your words: It is more blessed to give than to receive.

Like a city built on a hill, grant that my light will shine before others—so when they see my good works they may glorify my Father in heaven.

O Lord, let my affections be set on things above, not on things of this earth. Make me a faithful steward of your many gifts. Or if you prefer that my riches take wing and fly away, make me content in whatever situation I am in. May I always act like a stranger and pilgrim on earth, so that when my time comes I may praise you forever and ever.

Grant this, O Father, for your dear Son's sake, Jesus Christ our Lord. Amen and amen.

—*George Whitefield*

Come quickly and soon, Lord Jesus

Lord, we comfort ourselves with the prospect of a future when every evil and infirmity will cease. We know who said, "Surely I come quickly." And do not our hearts echo to your words? Do not the Spirit and the bride agree? Yes! Amen!

Even so, come Lord Jesus. Come and put an end to our fears and failings. Come and deliver us from this scene of strife and confusion. We are weary of living in the tents of this brutal world. We are weary of ourselves.

Oh! We can hardly bear to pass day after day with such faint, unworthy glimpses of your beauty and your goodness. We are weary and ashamed of our holy things. So much coldness and wandering in prayer, in reading the word, in your public ordinances, that we cannot help but say "Oh that I had wings like a dove, that I might fly far away from this vain ensnaring world!"

When will this conflict cease? When will all our tears be wiped away? When will we see you as you are, and be formed to resemble you more completely?

The time is short, and passing away quickly. We hold out a little longer, in faith and patience. You will come and not delay. In the meantime, may we have grace to improve the present, as the only opportunity we can have of glorifying you, our Lord and Savior, in a sinful world.

When we get safely home, we will not think we have done and suffered too much on the way.

I am yours.

Amen.

—*John Newton*

May we practice for heaven

"Your will be done, on earth as it is in heaven" (Matthew 6:10).

Lord, can such a thing really be? Reaching that goal seems so high, so heavenly, so impossible!

Yet if it were not within our reach, you would not have taught us to pray for it. Doing the will of God from the heart must be at least the reflection, the copy, of the perfect obedience of the saints in light.

Oh, to begin the service of heaven, while yet on earth! Practicing here, to be made perfect there! Learning the laws, manners, and customs of the land where our eternal inheritance awaits us!

May we diligently prepare ourselves for our citizenship in heaven. Amen.

—*Susannah Spurgeon*

I will see you one day

Lord, you might well say that "man shall not see me and live" (Exodus 33:20).

For when you display just one faint ray, or allow one glimpse of your glorious presence, this frail tabernacle is ready to crumble into dust before you.

But! One day I will be able to behold you, face to face. These eyes will see the glory, and they will gaze forever in complete joy.

For now, this corruptible clay cannot support itself under the weight of your love. But one day it will put on that freedom from corruption. One day I will be able to enjoy the full and eternal fruit of your glory. Amen.

—Hester Ann Roe Rogers

How I long for heaven

I love your house, Lord, the place where your honor dwells!

Let me continue and increase more and more in my love for you. Let me advance daily in this pilgrimage. As my soul pants for you, may it sanctify each day's labor and refresh my waking thoughts by night.

Let my heart be always where my treasure is. And in this desolate wilderness may I wish nothing other than to arrive at my heavenly promised land, and have a part in the society and joys of that happy people who have the Lord for their God.

Not that I dare presume to hope for your beauty and joy on my own account. Let the merit of him who died to purchase this mansion for me ... be applied to me. Let his intercession make up for my lack of worth, and then I am safe. Amen.

—Stephen Tyng

Your Will Be Done

Help me to remember your rule

You rule, O Lord. Your will be done. Keep me from being absorbed by, or too concerned with, worldly things. Help me to remember that Christians should regard and feel themselves as strangers and pilgrims. My portion, my conversation, my treasure, my country is in heaven.

May these also be my habitual feelings, through your grace, O Lord. Amen.

—William Wilberforce

Prepare us for duty as soldiers

Thank you, Lord, that you do not send us to battle at our own expense. And you always prepare us for any duties we are assigned.

Command us as you will. Whatever it is our duty to embrace, and however your call comes, help us to answer, "Here I am, send me!"

Help all your servants to know better your mission for them. May we be less concerned with making our own way, and more concerned with finding the way you have made for us. Amen.

—Alexander Maclaren

Help us to obey

O Lord, we bring you many sins for forgiveness. We do need your cleansing grace. We have fallen far beneath your purposes for us and have often gone directly against you.

Lord! We always suffer for breaking the commands you lay upon us. So in days to come may the deepest voice in our hearts be "Lord, what will you have me do?"

Thank you that you never leave such a question unanswered. May our ears be tuned to catch the whispers of your will, and so not need its thunders. May we dwell in you, and love the commander so much that we delight in all that he commands.

We pray for more of the kind of love in our hearts that fulfills the law. And we pray that you would open our hearts to your love, that it may motivate us to sweet and swift obedience. Amen.

—Alexander Maclaren

Let your will be ours

O Lord, may it be true of us that when we pray, it is not we that speak, but your Spirit in us. Breathe into our desires, so our prayers may be sweet and acceptable to you. After all, you have given the Spirit by which we pray.

We would not dictate to you, Lord. We would not bring our hot and foolish longings and wishes to your throne. We ask that deepest of all in us may be the Master's prayer: "Nevertheless, not my will, but yours, be done" (Luke 22:42).

Help us to live in peaceful submission and trust. Help us to accept what you appoint, and to be fellow-workers with you for our profit and growth in godliness. Lead us in paths of righteousness, to strengthen our feeble desires and resolves. May we run with patient perseverance the race which you appoint.

Forgive our imperfection, the blots and stains, and the interruptions or rebellions in our daily lives. Help us more and more to bring our whole being into union with you, so that you direct our thoughts, wishes, affections, purposes, efforts, and aims. Amen.

—Alexander Maclaren

We are both doing the same will

"Your will be done, on earth as it is in heaven" (Matthew 6:10).

My God, I bless you for the most welcome and soothing thought that, while the dear one you have taken is joyfully doing your will in heaven, I, by your tender grace, may be doing the same on earth.

I cannot do it as perfectly, but may I do it patiently, humbly, and acceptably. Lord, make this my daily desire and delight!

How near this hope brings me to my loved one—who is with Christ, and Christ is with me. There is only the veil of flesh between us, and that may be torn away any day soon. Then we will be together with him, amen.

—*Susannah Spurgeon*

You awakened me from death

Lord, when I leaned on a staff of my own devising, it betrayed me. It broke under me. It was not your staff.

Though I had resolved to be a god, you showed me that I was only a human. But since my own staff was broken, may I lay hold of yours?

O great God, you allowed me to live while I so dishonored you. You know everything. And it was your hand alone that could awaken me from the death in which I was, and was contented to be.

Not unto me. Count not a shadow of praise or merit to me. But let all the glory be given your most holy name! As surely as you made the mouth with which I pray, so surely you prompt every prayer of faith I utter.

You have made me all that I am, and given me all I have. Amen.

—Robert Murray M'Cheyne

School us, Lord

Dear Savior, we are your disciples, and you are teaching us the art of living. But we are very dull and very slow. There is a bias in our corrupt nature, there are poor examples in the world, and the influence of an ungodly generation shows even on those who know you.

Do not be impatient with us. School us at your feet until at last we learn some of the finest lessons of self-sacrifice, meekness, humility, fervor, boldness, and love.

Lord, educate us for a higher life, and let that life begin here. May we be always in the school, always disciples, and when we are out in the world may we put in practice what we have learned at the feet of Jesus. What he tells us in darkness may we proclaim in the light, and what he whispers in our ear in the closets may we sound forth upon the housetops.

Mold us into your image. Let us live in you and live like you. Let us gaze at your glory until we are transformed by the sight. Amen.

—Charles Spurgeon

When things get difficult

O Lord, you are a God of knowledge. Your understanding is infinite, and you are never at a loss to bring about what is best for us.

But you know our thoughts, Lord, and you know they are vain. We often do not know what to do for ourselves. At this time especially our affairs are tangled. We are confused. We cannot see how to free ourselves from our troubles.

But a person's goings are of the Lord. How then can we understand our own way? Our heart may advise his way, but the Lord directs our steps.

If we lean not on our own understanding, but in all our ways acknowledge you, you have promised to direct our paths. And when we commit our way to you, and trust in you, we have your word that you will bring it to pass.

So our eyes are on you, O God. We seek you now for wisdom to discern the path of duty. Without you, Lord, our wisdom is foolishness. Teach us which path to follow, and how to follow your will. We ask it for Jesus Christ's sake. Amen.

—*Charles Simeon and Benjamin Jenks*

I AM YOUR PROPERTY; SEND ME

Heavenly Father, here I am. You have bought me with a price. I am your property.

I renounce all claim to do my own will, all claim to govern my own life, all claim to have my own way.

I give myself up unreservedly to you—all I am and all I have. Take me and all I have, and do with me whatever you will. Send me wherever you will. Use me as you will.

I surrender myself and all I possess absolutely, unconditionally, forever, to your control and use. I am yours.

I am purchased by the precious blood of Christ. If you want me to serve overseas, make it clear to me and I will go.

Heavenly Father, I desire to know your will. I will do your will if you make it clear. But you are light and in you is no darkness at all. If this is your will make it clear as day and I will do it. Amen.

—*R. A. Torrey*

Let Us Hear Your Voice and Truth

Is that you knocking?

Lord, I humbly hope it is you knocking at the door of my heart. I hope you are the one calling forth these more than usually lively emotions of contrition, desire, faith, trust, and gratitude.

Oh may I hear your voice and open the door and let you in! Come in to relationship and fellowship. May I thrive as a believer, bringing forth abundant fruits of the Spirit to the glory of God.

O Lord, I am lost in astonishment at your mercy and love. I am amazed that you should not only quit the glory and happiness of heaven to be made man, and bear the most excruciating torments and bitter degradation for our deliverance and salvation—but also that you bear with us, even though we, knowing all your goodness, are still cold and insensible to it.

You strive with our perversity; you conquer our opposition. Even knowing ahead of time of our base ingratitude, you performed these miracles of mercy. You knew me and my hardness, and coldness, and my unworthy response to all your goodness when you called me out of the crowd. Still you shone into my heart with the light of the glory of God, in the face of Jesus Christ.

So we exclaim that as the heavens are higher than the earth, so are your ways higher than our ways, and your thoughts than our thoughts. O Lord, I cast myself before you. Do not refuse me, though I am unworthy of all your wonderful goodness.

Grant me more and more of humility, love, faith, and hope. Help me to long for complete renewal into your image. Help me and hear me, Lord. I come to you as my only Savior. Be my help, my strength, my peace, and joy, and consolation, my Alpha and Omega, my all in all. Amen.

—*William Wilberforce*

Unclose my ears

Cause me to hear, Lord. As you opened the eyes of Elisha's servant to see your armies of defense and protection for your prophet, unclose my ears so the tones of your still small voice may penetrate to my heart and thrill it with exceeding joy.

Or if I am too deafened by the roar and rush of earth's turmoil and distress, speak more loudly to me, Lord. Cause me to hear, in order that I would not miss the unspeakable privilege of listening to you. Amen.

—*Susannah Spurgeon*

Help me to know and love the truth

Lord, do not be angry with me for praying this way. But you know I have always sought the truth. I have earnestly prayed that you would lead me to the truth, and that I would be rooted, established, and built up in the truth. The truth is in Jesus!

Now today I want to solemnly renew my prayer to you, and enter afresh into covenant with you.

Lord God, I find myself in a world where thousands profess your name. Some preach, some write, and some talk about religion. Everyone says they seek the truth. They say they have Jesus on their side.

But I am afraid of being turned away from the simplicity of the gospel. I feel as if my understanding is full of darkness. My reasoning is so imperfect. My will is ready to stray, and my passions volatile.

Illuminate my understanding. Teach reason to my reasoning, and steadfastness to my will. Let every faculty I possess be kept within the bounds of your service.

Do not let the clever craftiness of the wicked draw me aside. Do not let me even misguide myself.

Lord, you have given me a determination to accept no secondhand teaching, but to search for everything at the pure fountain of your word. Yet I am afraid. I am just as prone to make mistakes as anyone, prone to be led away from truth by my own imagination.

You have promised that "he leads the humble in what is right, and teaches the humble his way" (Psalm 25:9). Lord, you know my heart is humble. Guide me by your counsel and receive me to glory.

I pray also that I may not only be kept back from error, but that I may so love the truth as never to keep it back. O Lord, never let me preach holiness while neglecting the truths of your word. Holy practice depends on sacred principle.

Open my eyes to see the wonders of your word, Lord, and let me feel their transforming tendency. And let my tongue stick to the roof of my mouth if I ever fail to declare what I know to be the whole counsel of God. Amen.

—Andrew Fuller

Keep us in truth

Almighty God, you have sent the Spirit of truth to guide us into all truth. Now rule our lives by your power in such a way that we may always be truthful in thought, word, and deed.

Keep us and protect us so that no fear or hope would ever make us false in speech or actions. Cast out from us anything that leads to or loves a lie. And bring us all into the perfect freedom of your truth, through Jesus Christ, your Son, our Lord. Amen.

—B. F. Westcott

We Want to Be Holy

We are all different—and loved

Father, we all come out of very different circumstances. Our day's work, trials, and joys are diverse. But we thank you that in all this infinite variety and complexity of circumstances and events which make up our lives you seek the same ends with us all. You express the same love that embraces us all.

And so we thank you for all the ways by which you lead us. In all these things help us to recognize your loving-kindness.

Deliver us from the many things in ourselves which contradict your will. And show us more clearly the loftiness and greatness of the possibilities of your grace in Jesus Christ. Show us your love for each of us.

Help us to make holiness our highest joy as well as our binding duty. Help us to be perfect as our Father in heaven is perfect (Matthew 5:48). And forgetting the things that are behind, may we "press on toward the goal for the prize for the upward call of God in Christ Jesus" (Philippians 3:14). Amen.

—Alexander Maclaren

Show me how to be holy

My God, save me from the peace which is no peace. And let me have no peace either without my Savior or with my sins.

Save me from moral lethargy, O God. May I never escape remorse until I am once and for all sealed unto him—the only one in whom I am safe.

And as the very God of peace, sanctify me wholly. Let me know both peace and the pursuit of holiness, with all earnestness and honesty, but without the anxiety of a legalistic spirit. May the law of the spirit of life in Christ Jesus set me free from the law of sin and death.

Let me bear the burdens of others. And save me from the self-centered laziness that would keep me from serving others.

But above all, let me live in holy abstinence from sin, even in the least appearance and degree of it. It may not be my besetting sin to tamper with the limits of integrity, but save me from tampering with all limits.

I confess, O Lord, my grievous delinquency from holiness of heart and life. Lay me under that most sacred and special obligation to be holy, even as Christ is holy. Amen.

—Thomas Chalmers

What keeps me from holiness?

Father, you know that I covet earnestly the loveliness of sanctification. I want to obey your command to be holy. And if a longing for complete surrender to you would secure this special grace, I would have it already.

So what is it that constantly defeats my purpose, foils my efforts, and prevents me from receiving my most devout desire?

Dear Master, if your will concerning me is my sanctification, why is that will not more absolutely done in me? Can it be that I am unconsciously cherishing something in my heart that hinders the work of your Holy Spirit, so the blessing you have designed for me does not reach me because the way is barred by a will not wholly yielded to yours?

Or have I been satisfying myself with mere empty desires for conformity to Christ? Have I been indulging in poor feeble longings in which there was so much half-heartedness that the Spirit of God was grieved, and would not reveal his power?

O Lord, pity me and pardon me! Awaken my soul to an earnest sense of the solemn responsibility involved in belonging to you, and bearing your name! Rouse in me, Lord, a blessed eagerness to become all that you wish me to be.

Fill me with that mighty influence which works in us "both to will and to work" for your good pleasure (Philippians 2:13). Chasten and afflict me, Lord, if nothing else will serve to make me a partaker of your holiness.

Dear Father, I must have this blessing. Help me to pray intelligently, remembering that awful cost you have paid to answer, and glorifying you for the matchless love which makes me, as the hymn reminds us, "With his spotless vesture on, holy as the Holy One." Amen.

—Susannah Spurgeon

I AM WEAK BUT WILLING

My body is still weak, though on the recovery. Lord, if you would be pleased to raise me up, let it be to do more good. I desire to live only for this!

Lord, I am yours, to serve you forever with soul and body, time and talents.

My God, now all I am and have is devoted to you. In your mercy and by your grace, help me to persevere in all well-doing. Amen.

—Francis Asbury

A rebel's prayer

O my Father, I ask for life—but deserve death. I have been disloyal to my king—but yet have the confidence to fly to him for protection. I have despised my judge—but look to him for relief. I have plugged my ears against my Father's commands—but depend on him for his affection and care.

Sadly, my feet run swiftly toward ruin, but are slow in the way that leads to life and safety. I run toward sickness, wounds, and death. And I take no care to avoid the darts which caused those wounds, even when I feel the sting. But I only notice them when they bring me to the edge of the grave.

And those maladies which the spiritual physician had cured? I bring them back on myself. What good can be expected for the futile remorse of that sinner who commits evil, and repents of it, and then does the same evil again? This is a mortifying thought to me, having so often returned with the dog to the vomit.

I cannot remember how often I have offended you. But this I own with a heavy heart: I have taught others by my example how to sin. Yet despite my poor memory, I must still deal with a just and terrible judge.

So I beg you, by your tender mercies, pour balm into my wounds to counteract the venom of my diseases. Restore me to spiritual health. Let me drink of your heavenly sweetness and love the taste so much that I will no longer relish the world's sensual delights.

Instead may I despise its pleasures and cheerfully take on life's afflictions. May I fix my heart on true, noble joys. May I disdain those empty, transitory shadows that flesh and blood is so foolishly fond of and so fearful of losing.

What can the world give, without you? Let it be counted like dung. Do not allow me to hide behind flimsy excuses or indulge in doing what I ought not. Without question, let me hate whatever displeases you. And let me eagerly wish for (and pursue) whatever you love.

Let me feel no satisfaction in any joys without you. Let me not hold back from any sufferings for you. And let the mention of your name always refresh me.

Let tears be my daily food, so I may attain your righteousness. Let my single aim be to serve you. Pardon my sins for your mercy's sake, keep my ears open to the voice of your way, and incline my heart away from evil. Amen.

—Stephen Tyng

A PRAYER FOR HOLINESS IN THE WORKPLACE

Lord, you see how much in the daily course of my business and employment I am in danger of being led to think profit is the one thing.

O my God, save me from the snare of covetousness. Do not let the enchantment of riches destroy me, nor honors or pleasures entice me. Let me see them as the fleeting vanities they are, and may I look forward to the day when they cannot profit at all.

Rivet upon my mind the everlasting value of your love and the comforts of your Spirit. Help me remember the blessings of obedience and faith in Christ Jesus, so that in the midst of all my gains I will receive that treasure which will never fail.

And in order that business may not destroy my soul, grant me a perpetual suspicion of its tendency to extinguish in me all sense of spiritual blessings and alienate my heart from God.

I know how many thousands have been swallowed up and lost in pursuit of their work. I have seen the world intent only upon amassing wealth. And I have felt the same passion kindling within my own corrupted heart. So God, in your mercy and by your dear Son's blood, put your Spirit within me. Cause me to use this world, not abuse it. Help me to use moderation even in the midst of diligent application to my calling.

Never allow me to be so immersed in trade or merchandise as to make me cold and formal in prayer or a stranger to the peace and joys of the faithful. Help me not to ignore my holy duties or your Sabbath, or to turn away from opportunities for devotion. Because that is how my soul can be kept alive to God and grace obtained to withstand sin.

If riches increase, grant that in the same proportion I may be liberal to the poor and needy. Possess my mind with a sense of your presence, wherever I am and whatever I do. May I never act with deceit or lies.

Keep me, Lord, so that neither the cares nor the pleasures of this world, nor the deceitfulness of riches, nor the lusting after things, may ever prevail against me or make me dishonor my Christian testimony. May I never sell my soul for that which perishes in the using.

Hear me, O Lord, for Jesus Christ's sake, who died to deliver us from the power of this present evil world, even as he was not of the world. To him, with you, O Father and the Holy Spirit, be all honor and glory now and for evermore. Amen.

—Henry Venn

Keep me from spiritual shipwreck, Lord

Lord, you are the beautiful gate of heaven, the door at which the sheep must enter. But sadly we lie groveling here below, our souls clutching the dust.

Stretch out your hand and raise us up. Strengthen our weakness, so we may serve with courage in this spiritual war. Of ourselves we are not able to stand against the force that comes against us. Help us against our enemies' power. Help us against our own negligence and cowardice, and defend us from the treachery of our own unfaithful hearts.

We are so frail, weak, and deserving of contempt. We are slaves to excess and lust, and we avoid virtue. And yet, helpless as we are, when we come under your banner, borne up by your cross, we are buoyed up by faith. Then we can commit ourselves boldly to this great sea, filled with reefs and other uncounted dangers on which the careless and unbelieving shipwreck their vessels.

Intercede for me, therefore, most gracious Savior. By your powerful intervention and all-sufficient merit may I be able to bring this vessel and its cargo safe to shore—to the haven of peace, salvation, and never-ending joy. Amen.

—Stephen Tyng

We want to be a cleansed temple

Sadly, we are sometimes subject to unbelief. If unexpected trials come, or if the body grows faint, we are liable to doubt the faithful promise and so grieve the Holy Spirit. Lord, we cannot bear this! We cannot bear this! It is not enough for us that our clothes are clean, or that we walk uprightly before others. We long to walk before you in such a way that there will be nothing to grieve your Spirit, nothing to frustrate the tender love of our Beloved.

Come, divine Spirit, exercise your cleansing power. I pray that everything might help us toward purity, for we crave it. There is groaning within us to be utterly delivered from the things of the flesh. In spirit, soul, and body, we want to be a cleansed temple fit for the indwelling of the Holy One of Israel.

Lord, help us in our daily life to be as Christ was. If we are people of sorrows, may there be that radiance about our sorrow which there was about his in patience and holy submission to the divine law. If we are people of activity, may our activity be like his, for "he went about doing good" (Acts 10:38). May we seek in all ways the good of others and the glory of our God.

Bless us in our example and influence. May there be a sweetness and light about us that is impossible to miss. And we crave this not for our own honor, but that our light may so shine before others, so that they may see our good works and give glory to our Father who is in heaven (Matthew 5:16). Lord grant us this! Amen.

—Charles Spurgeon

Help Us to Trust You in Faith

You still answer prayer, Jesus

You have never changed—dear, faithful, covenant-keeping Jesus—always ever just the same. Your ear is not heavy that you cannot hear, nor is your arm shortened that you cannot save.

O blessed Jesus, we dare to trust you. We dare to believe your word. We are walking to meet you on the waters, like Peter, today. And while we keep our eyes on you, you will not let us fall.

Put faith in our heart, Lord, meet the expectations of your people, that all may know our God still lives and answers prayers, in Jesus's name, amen.

—Aimee Semple McPherson

Let me walk in Abraham's footsteps of faith

My God, help me to rejoice in the light of that now-risen day which made Abraham glad when he saw it from afar.

May Christ be precious to me, he who is the sun of righteousness, with healing under his wings.

Let me see the same invitation that was in the first call of Abraham, for the sake of all the families of the earth, a great purpose of mercy for all humanity. For you say, "Turn to me and be saved, all the ends of the earth!" (Isaiah 45:22).

Help me walk in the footsteps of the faith of my father Abraham. He left it all behind to follow your voice.

Gracious Father, arm me with the same kind of attitude. Show me, at all times, the path of duty. May I surrender all that is dear, whenever you require the sacrifice. Give me a firm and honest resolve, and then I will feel the sweetness of unreserved obedience.

May your will, without limit and without exception, be my will. Then your glory will shine on my ways. Amen.

—Thomas Chalmers

No excuse for our unbelief

Dear master, you come to each one of us with the same question as that which shamed your timid disciples: "Where is your faith?"

And we are silent before you, Lord. We have no excuse to offer for our unbelief. We have not even the slightest excuse they had when they scarcely realized that you were God incarnate, when they asked among themselves, "What sort of man is this?"

We know you as the once crucified but now risen Lord. All power in heaven and on earth has been given you. And you may well marvel at our unbelief. Amen.

—Susannah Spurgeon

Give me the heart of a child

O my Father, teach me to realize how deep and strong is the love of your heart to me, since it led you to give your only begotten son, Jesus Christ himself, to redeem me and bring me home to you!

Help me realize everything this wonderful relationship means to me. As your child, I may claim all that you have promised to give. And if I am living and acting as your child—dwelling with you, loving you, and obeying you—I will surely find that your fatherly love is ready to grant every reasonable desire of my heart.

Dear Lord, when I see earthly fathers whose love for their little ones is intense, forbearing, and unspeakably tender, I feel ashamed that I do not better understand the love of your heart toward me, your child through faith in Christ Jesus!

I cannot work out such a sum, Lord. But I know the love must be infinitely greater, closer, and dearer. Because you are the infinite God, and your love is from everlasting.

Oh, that I may have the spirit of a child when I draw near to you! Amen.

—Susannah Spurgeon

Help us to trust like children

Blessed Lord! Though it is one of the first, simplest, and most glorious lessons in your school, you know this is to our hearts one of the hardest to learn:

We know so little of the love of the Father.

Lord! Teach us to live with the Father in such a way that his love may be to us nearer, clearer, and dearer than the love of any earthly father. And let the assurance of his hearing our prayer be as much greater than the confidence in an earthly parent, as the heavens are higher than earth, or as God is infinitely greater than man.

Lord! Show us that it is only our unchildlike distance from the Father that hinders the answer to prayer. And lead us on to the true life of God's children.

Lord Jesus! It is fatherlike love that wakens childlike trust. Reveal to us the Father and his tender, pitying love, so that we may become childlike and experience how the power of prayer lies in this child-life.

Blessed Son of God! The Father loves you and has given you all things. And you love the Father and have done all things he commanded you. So you have the power to ask all things.

Lord! Give us your own Spirit, the Spirit of the Son. Make us childlike, as you were on earth. And let every prayer be breathed in the faith that as heaven is higher than earth, so God's Father-love and his readiness to give us what we ask surpasses all we can think or conceive. Amen.

—Andrew Murray

You Deserve All the Credit

O Jesus, if you speak one word of peace, that will establish in me an everlasting calm.

Fill me with your love now. Accept me, I pray, and use me a little for your glory. I have done nothing for you yet, and I would like to do something. Accept me and my service, and you take all the glory.

Help me to resign all to your will, with complete reliance on your powerful hand. I lean on your word alone. I commit my way unto you. I trust in you, that you will direct my steps. Amen.

—David Livingstone

I cling to your lifebelt

"Not that we have loved God, but that he loved us" (1 John 4:10). These blessed words seep into my dull and aching heart, dear Lord, and I thank you for them. You have taken them from your own book and spoken them to me with your living, loving voice, and they have brought me alive.

With shame and sorrow, I had brought to you a hard and insensible heart. I could only groan out before you my utter lack of faith and feeling. The very desire to love you seemed to lie chained and powerless within me, with only an occasional struggle revealing its bare existence.

Then, Lord, while I knelt in your presence with bowed head and troubled spirit, tears and sighs my only prayers, you whispered those sweet words in my ear. They brought light and liberty to my captive soul.

I bless your dear name for this glorious deliverance! It is not my poor, cold, half-hearted love which satisfies and comforts me. It is your love—great, full, and free, eternal as you yourself!

Surely I had known this before, Lord. But I had shut myself up in unbelief until, in your sweet mercy, you spoke the word that released me from my bonds, opened my prison doors, and let me out into the sunshine of true peace in believing.

"Not that we have loved God." No, and that is the sad wonder and mystery of our unrenewed life. Not to have loved you is our greatest guilt and shame. And it was even worse, for we were enemies. We had put ourselves in an attitude of defiance against our best friend. Or if not openly defiant, we were totally forgetful of him to whom we owed our heart's allegiance.

"Not that we have loved God." Dearest Lord, you know how deeply and sadly true this was of me, and how I mourn over the years spent without love to you, at a distance from you. O hard heart, O blind eyes, O dull, sluggish soul that could be unmindful of the strivings of God's Spirit. That could deliberately neglect the pleadings of a Savior's love, and see no beauty in the one who is altogether lovely.

"But that he loved us." Here is a blessed contrast, the antidote for sin's sting. Here is light after darkness, hope after despair, life after death! Lord, my soul flings itself on this glorious fact, this saving truth, as a drowning person seizes a lifebelt thrown in the surging sea!

If you do not love me and lift me, I perish forever. But there is no question of sinking when Jesus saves, no fear of losing life when he loves. O my Lord, how I thank you for this precious word upon which you have caused me to hope! Now, all day long, my heart will sing over the safety and blessedness of being freely loved, instead of fretting about the sad lack of my poor love to you.

"Not that we loved God" is darkness, bitterness, and eternal death. But "that he loved us" is light and pardon, peace and everlasting life. Amen.

—*Susannah Spurgeon*

And you reply: My kindness

"My kindness." Dear Lord, the words are sweet to my soul as honey. They carry an answer to all my misgivings, a response to all my pleas, and a promise of power to overcome all my weakness.

I sometimes say to you, "Lord, how is it that you can be so tender and indulgent to one so forgetful, so unworthy, so inexcusable as I am?"

And your answer is: My kindness. "I have loved you with an everlasting love" (Jeremiah 31:3).

"But Lord, I am a worse and greater sinner than I thought I was. Every day reveals to me some undiscovered evil in my heart, which must be displeasing in your sight."

Again you say: My kindness. "I will not remember your sins" (Isaiah 43:25).

"But Lord, I have no power to do right, and I cannot of myself even think a good thought, much less live that life of holiness which you require."

And again you give me that sweet reply: My kindness. "My grace is sufficient for you, for my power is made perfect in weakness" (2 Corinthians 12:9).

If only I had a pen dipped in the praises of heaven to write what your loving-kindness and tender mercy have been to me!

"My steadfast love shall not depart from you" (Isaiah 54:10). Loving Lord, let the comfort of this precious "shall not ..." sink deep into my soul. May it strengthen me to face every difficulty, resist every evil, and bear any trial. Make it be a sweet resting place and refuge for me, Lord, where I may be sheltered from all the disturbing changes of the world around me.

Friends may grow cold, times and circumstances may change, old age may creep on, infirmities may gather themselves together, and flesh and heart may fail. My feet may touch the cold waters of the river of death. Even so, this promise will stand fast and true, and your kindness will not depart from me forever, for it will present me "blameless before the presence of his glory with great joy" (Jude 24).

Amen.

—Susannah Spurgeon

We can meet you in the cross

We have stood under the peal of thunder, Lord. And we trembled. The lightning flash revealed our sin and made us cry for shelter.

We have watched your march through history, and there have been traces of blood and tears behind on your track. And as we look out into the eternal future our hearts stand still.

We are just leaves in the great forest of existence, or bursting bubbles upon the mighty ocean of being.

But when we come to see that your ideal is in the divine man who died for us, we fear you no more, but approach with the confidence of a little child.

For if you love the man Christ Jesus, and we love him too, we can meet you in the cross with its dying agony.

It is a great encouragement to know that God's ideal—your ideal—is the man who died. Amen.

—F. B. Meyer

Keep Us in Your Word

Give us faith to believe your word

O Lord, your word is truth, and we thank you for the Bible. We thank you that we can read it and hear it.

Your word is better than all other books. It converts the soul and makes wise the simple-minded. It makes the heart rejoice. It tells us the greatest things and the best things.

Give us grace to love your word and to do what it requires.

Give us your Holy Spirit to open our eyes, that we may see clearly what your will is. In mercy give us faith, that we may believe with our hearts all that you have spoken.

We ask all for Christ's sake. Amen.

—William Swan Plumer

A prayer before reading the Bible

O God, here and now I give myself up to you—for you to command me and lead me, to shape me, send me, and do with me absolutely as you will.

Make me a little child, O God. Empty me of my own notions. Teach me your own mind. Make me ready like a little child to receive all that you have to say, no matter how contrary it is to what I have thought up to now. Amen.

—R. A. Torrey

Help us to study your word

By your providence, blessed Lord, all the holy Scriptures were written and preserved to teach us. Now grant us the grace to study those Scriptures each day with patience and love. Strengthen our souls with the fullness of their divine teaching.

In the process, keep us from all pride and irreverence. Guide us in the deep things of your heavenly wisdom. And in your great mercy lead us by your word into everlasting life, through Jesus Christ our Savior, amen.

—B. F. Westcott

Keep me in the word

Lord, instead of finding my great delight in the Bible, I am often glad when I can lay it down and take up something else. What a cold, dull, earthly heart I have!

Quicken me, I pray. Cleanse and raise my desires. Give me your Spirit to make me take more pleasure in what concerns you, and in what you in your love have written for me.

I want to be yours. Make me what you would have me, and what I wish to be. Amen.

—William Henry Ridley

Teach Us to Pray

Why do my prayers fall short?

O Lord Jesus! Teach me to understand and believe what you have promised. Whatever reasonings my heart seeks to satisfy itself with when no answer comes are not hidden from you.

Sometimes I think my prayer is not in harmony with the Father's secret counsel. Or I think perhaps you would give me something better, or that prayer as fellowship with God is blessing enough without an answer.

And yet, blessed Lord, I find in your teaching on prayer that you did not speak of these things. You said so plainly that prayer may and must expect an answer. You assure us that this is the fellowship of a child with the Father: the child asks and the Father gives.

Blessed Lord! Your words are faithful and true. It must be because my prayers are faulty that my experience of answered prayer is not clearer. It must be because I live too little in the Spirit, that my prayer is too little in the Spirit, and that the power for the prayer of faith is lacking.

Lord! Teach me to pray. Lord Jesus! I trust you for it. Teach me to pray in faith. Lord! Teach me this lesson of today: everyone who asks, receives. Amen.

—Andrew Murray

Make us one, Lord

Blessed Lord, you prayed so earnestly for the unity of your people. Teach us how you invite and urge us to this unity by your precious promise given to united prayer. It is when we are one in love and desire that our faith has your presence and the Father's answer.

O Father! We pray for your people, and for every smaller circle of those who meet together, that they may be one. Remove all selfishness and self-interest, all narrowness of heart and estrangement by which that unity is hindered.

Cast out the spirit of the world and the flesh, through which your promise loses all its power.

O let the thought of your presence and the Father's favor draw us all nearer to each other.

Grant especially that your church may believe that it is by the power of united prayer that she can bind and loose in heaven, that Satan can be cast out, that souls can be saved, that mountains can be removed, that the kingdom can be hastened.

And grant, good Lord, that in the circle with which I pray, the prayer of the church may indeed be the power through which your name and word are glorified. Amen.

—*Andrew Murray*

Give us a spirit of prayer

Merciful and gracious God, draw us by your Holy Spirit to the devout exercise of prayer. Convince us of our guilt and weakness, our blindness and depravity, so that with great earnestness we may cry unto you.

But do not let our prayer be a mere lip service or offered only to pacify conscience. May it be the hunger and thirst of our soul after you. And as you know the great corruption of our hearts, help us understand there is no higher affront to your name than to live without prayer.

Prepare us to pray. Convince us that if we regard iniquity in our heart, you will not hear us. But if we call upon you in truth, you will hear, and bless.

In all our prayer, may we draw close with a contrite heart and humble spirit. May a sense of our sin, a knowledge of your infinite purity, and a conviction of the distance between sinners and the eternal God fill our souls with humility.

May we never dare to approach you in our own name, trusting in our own goodness. May we always look in all our prayers to Jesus, who endured the cross, and ever lives to make intercession.

Help us to esteem prayer as our highest privilege, and be more and more fervent and diligent until all our prayers are answered and changed into everlasting praise.

And as we beg for the spirit of prayer, we request also what is equally necessary: a love of your blessed word. Teach us the true meaning and interpretation. Let us not lean on our own understanding. Give us delight in reading your word and pondering it in our hearts. And as we read, may we drink deep into its spirit and be molded by it.

Hear our prayer, and do abundantly far above all we can ask or think, through Jesus Christ our Lord. Amen.

—Henry Venn

Give Us Peace and Your Spirit

The waiting game

Blessed Master, I thank you for my waiting times. They are times of love and favor. They draw me nearer, closer, and more urgently to your feet.

Your delays are not denials. When you seem slow to answer prayer, it is only to make me more eager for the mercy, or to teach me to ask with greater confidence, or that you may gather up your blessings in order to bestow them "far more abundantly than all that we ask or think" (Ephesians 3:20).

"My soul waits for the Lord" (Psalm 130:6). Ah, Lord—what special blessedness of sweet content I find in waiting before you when you fill my heart with adoring love and gratitude, when I am silent. No words are needed between you and my wondering soul. When I am humbled to the very dust by your love and favor, yet lifted into the heavenly places through Christ Jesus.

And so I wait, and watch, and worship. This is the waiting upon you which renews the strength of my spiritual life. This is the waiting that never wearies, the expectancy that never disappoints, the hope that "does not put us to shame" (Romans 5:5).

Oh, to be found waiting at the gate. Waiting for God, and upon God, "until he comes" (1 Corinthians 11:26). Amen!

—Susannah Spurgeon

A request for the gift of the Holy Spirit

Heavenly Father, I come to you for the gift of your Spirit for service. I want it above everything else. O God, give me the Spirit! Empty me of self and of self-seeking. Bring me down into the dust before you, so that I may be filled with the Holy Spirit!

God of Elijah, I pray that a double portion of your Spirit may come upon me, that I may be anointed to do the work you have for me to do. We know that I have just a little while to stay here. In a few months or years, at longest, I will be gone. O God, help me to bear fruit while I live! May I no longer live in this lukewarm state. May I no longer toil day after day and month after month, and see no fruit.

Jesus, Master, you have gone up on high. You have led captivity captive. You are at the right hand of God, and you have power. Give us power! You can quicken us into new life. You can give us a fresh anointing. I pray you will do it today. Breathe upon us a breath from heaven.

Grant that I may know what it is to have the Holy Spirit resting upon me for service. I ask it all in the name and for the sake of your blessed Son. Amen.

—D. L. Moody

I want the Holy Spirit

Heavenly Father, we desire the Holy Spirit. You have said in your word, "If you then, who are evil, know how to give good gifts to your children, how much more will the heavenly Father give the Holy Spirit to those who ask him!" (Luke 11:13).

And you said again in Acts 2:39 that "the promise is for you and your children and for all who are far off, everyone whom the Lord our God calls to himself."

I am called; I am saved; and here I have your word for it. You have promised it. I ask you now to fill me with the Holy Spirit.

And Father, this is the confidence that I have toward you, that if I ask anything according to your will, you hear me. And if I know that you hear me in whatever I ask, I know that I have the requests that I have asked of you (1 John 5:14–15).

So I rise up and stand on this promise of God, and I say "It is mine." And it will be mine. Amen.

—R. A. Torrey

I PRAY FOR THE GIFT OF THE SPIRIT

Father in heaven, you sent your Son to reveal yourself to us. You sent your Father-love and all that love has for us. And the gift above all gifts which you would bestow in answer to prayer is the Holy Spirit.

O my Father! I come to you with this prayer: There is nothing I would desire so much as to be filled with the Holy Spirit. The blessings he brings are so unspeakable, and just what I need.

He sheds abroad your love in the heart, and fills it with yourself. I long for this.

He breathes the mind and life of Christ in me so that I live as he did, in and for the Father's love. I long for this.

He endues with power from on high for all my walk and work. I long for this.

O Father! I pray that you would give me this day the fullness of your Spirit. I ask this, resting on the words of my Lord: "How much more ... the Holy Spirit" (Luke 11:13). I do believe you hear my prayer.

I receive now what I ask, Father! I receive the gift this day. My Father works through the Spirit as he has promised. The Father delights to breathe his Spirit into his waiting child. Amen.

—*Andrew Murray*

Give me living water

O weary man, footsore and sorrowful, asking for a drink of water at the hands of a sinful woman, you are my Lord and redeemer.

I believe in you, I love you, I worship you! Nearly two thousand years have passed since you spoke the sweet words which now comfort my heart. Yet with what power and blessing they come to me now.

"If you knew" (John 4:10). Lord, you have told me who you are. In mercy you have revealed yourself to me. I know you to be that blessed gift of God which alone can save and satisfy my soul.

The depth of heaven's love is revealed in you. And you have shown me not only my need, but how your grace and power are enough to meet it. I am an empty sinner; you are a full Christ.

You have heard my heart's constant cry: "Lord, give me this living water." It is you I want, Lord. My soul thirsts for you. Not your gifts, nor your grace, nor even your glory could satisfy the desire of a soul which you have made to long for yourself.

You, the giver of all other precious things, are yourself the choicest gift. Lord, into the thirst of my empty heart pour the full stream of your living love. Give me yourself, or I die!

And, having asked, I believe that you do give, for you said "he would have given ..." (John 4:10). And I whisper softly to myself the blessed words: "who loved me and gave himself for me" (Galatians 2:20). I realize the sacred, overflowing joy of pardoned sin, and peace with God that fills and satisfies my soul.

So, dear Lord, my spirit, like a weary bird, folds its wings beside this sweet wellspring of comfort, creeps into this blessed "cleft of the rock" (Exodus 33:22), and is at rest. Amen.

—Susannah Spurgeon

Let the Spirit come, Lord

While the Spirit still strives with me, O God, let him no longer strive in vain.

I invite him to my heart—let him dwell there. I plead your own promise. I pray for this gift beyond measure. May it be planted completely in my heart, and may I become a temple of the Holy Spirit.

Without him I am totally and completely evil, in every thought and imagination, and continually. So let me hold out no longer. Help me to drop all resistance to his efforts, lest I so grieve him as to quench him. Lest I grieve him even as God was so grieved by the wickedness of people before the flood. Lest I provoke him to abandon me, leaving me unreclaimed and outcast from the presence of God, from the hopes and joys of eternity.

Heavenly Father, may I find grace in your eyes. And then may I invite and increase that grace. May I move ahead in the gospel economy—to those who have, more is given.

May I be faithful in that which I have, and so look and pray for more. The Holy Spirit is given to those who obey him. Let me make the right use of his influence, that I may be led to larger and ever-brightening examples of his presence.

Because the one who is faithful in that which is least will be counted worthy of a larger confidence. Amen.

—*Thomas Chalmers*

A PRAYER FOR PEACE

The still, small voice of the Savior's gospel is drowned by military music and the din of arms.

But the weapons of our warfare are not of this world.

Blessed Lord Jesus, when will you beat these swords into ploughs? When will sinful, guilty, dying mortals stop hurrying each other into the eternal world? When will we follow your blessed example, and work to save life—not destroy it? Amen.

—Alexander Viets Griswold

Make us still, Lord

God our Father, we want to make our life a song. We cannot say many words to you, but we want to live so that sweet music comes up to you from us, when our lives are in perfect union and accord with your nature.

Breathe your Spirit into us as we kneel before you. Subdue the selfishness that makes discord and unite our hearts in the one fear of your name.

May circumstances have no power to change the sweetness and beauty of our inner life. Day and night may we offer ourselves to you as a sweet-smelling sacrifice.

We thank you that we are full of need. We have learned that you give power to the faint and to those that have no power. A thorn in the flesh gives you an opportunity of perfecting the strength of Christ. You make your home with those with a humble and contrite spirit, who tremble at your word.

So take our weakness up into your strength. Take our ignorance into your wisdom. Take our changefulness into your everlasting constancy. Make us quiet. We chafe and fret and fill our lives with noise and bustle. We expend ourselves on many things that distract and weary us. Our voices, motions, and impulsiveness often point to the storm and unrest within.

Make us still in the depths of our nature. Make us quiet and peaceful. May we go to and fro among others with gentleness, patience, and endurance. May we live in the spirit of prayer.

We sometimes catch a glimpse of a life in which the heart goes out to you the entire day—when we smile to you in joy, confide to you in sorrow, and discuss with you all the details of daily life. In your grace, make that life always ours. Holy Spirit, teach us how to abide in Christ. Prompt us hour by hour to stay in fellowship with him.

We thank you for the Son of your love—for all he has done for us and will do. For all that he has been to us and will be. We know that he holds us in his strong pierced hand, that he loves us with the love that cannot let us go. We know that we are one with him in a union which nothing can break. We cannot realize what all this means, but we bless you and ask you to enable us to live as those compelled by such love, not to live to ourselves but to him.

Show us our part in the great harvest field and help us to fulfill it. Give grace, wisdom, and strength to those who are engaged in conflict against impurity. Hasten the reign of our blessed Lord. Be very near to us and all the members of our family. Supply our needs according to your riches in glory. We ask in the name of Jesus Christ. Amen.

—*F. B. Meyer*

We Lift Our Families and Young Ones to You

A PRAYER FOR MY FAMILY AND HOME

O God, help me to do right by my family by taking seriously my influence or even responsibility for their eternal destiny. Give me the happiness of a Christian family. Whatever happens in this world, may we possess the only true riches and be prepared for a heavenly inheritance of glory.

Then I will indeed have the blessing of Abraham, having God himself for the everlasting portion of me and mine.

We say of the one who is present everywhere, "Surely the Lord is in this place." And the world is the gateway to eternity. May this home be to us a school of preparation for heaven, for those mansions which never fall or decay.

My God, you know how much undue attention I give to a house built with hands, which I try to make into an earthly paradise. Be pleased though to let us live here in peace, a secure and comfortable home—and also a home fully dedicated to you.

But prepare me for the whole of your will. Enable me to keep a loose connection to the world, and not set my affections upon it. Let me feel that here I am just a stranger and a pilgrim, and that my actions plainly declare that I seek a country on the other side of death.

Help me in all this, good Lord. Amen.

—*Thomas Chalmers*

Prayer for an unsaved father

God, you hear my prayer, even amidst uncounted choirs of angels forever glorifying you and singing your praise. You hear the softest breathing of a prayerful, downtrodden heart. Now allow the prayers of a child for a beloved parent to come up before you.

My earthly father gave me life here in this world. In your providence he has tenderly watched over me and tried to make me happy.

In grateful return, Lord, would you enable me to be the humble means of leading him to you?

Let us thirst and come together to the waters, and "buy wine and milk without money and without price" (Isaiah 55:1).

Grant, Lord, that before we both die, our united voices may ascend to you in praise and blessing. Grant that we may together call upon the name of him who has redeemed us by his most precious blood, that in that blood our many sins may be washed away. Amen.

—Clara Lucas Balfour, quoting Amelia Opie

A wedding day dedication

Our gracious Lord God, we humbly pray you would accept this solemn surrender.

Unto you we give up our whole selves, bodies, soul, and spirits. We give all we have and all we are to you—to you altogether and entirely. Accept our surrender and sacrifice in and through the Son of your love!

And may we, by the help of your almighty power and goodness, show forth your praise continually, not only with our lips but in our lives. Lord, help us so to do.

Bless my most beloved husband and me in our new relation to each other. O bless us, bless us, bless us. May we be yours altogether, yours now, from now on and forevermore!

And my dearest Lord, accept my most grateful thanks for providing for me in your infinite wisdom and goodness such a precious follower of yours. Make me a worthy supporter and encourager. Let me not be a hindrance, but in your love and mercy a furtherance in every work of faith and labor of love.

And give us continually such degrees of grace that whether we live, we may live unto the Lord, or whether we die, we may die unto the Lord. So that living and dying we may be yours, O God, eternally yours!

Amen and amen.

—Penelope Coke

A PRAYER FOR THE CHILDREN

Heavenly Father, we pray that your blessing may rest upon words that may have been spoken in weakness. May they be carried home to our hearts with power.

Help us as parents to labor for the salvation of our children, that they may be with us in glory and not one of them missing when you come. Spare them as a father spares his own son. May we have the joy of seeing them come in the morning of their lives and give themselves to you.

And we pray for their Sunday school teachers. May their hearts be burdened for their scholars. May they plead with the children to come to Christ.

O Father! For Jesus Christ's sake hear our prayer. May we not rest day or night until we see those around us brought to the kingdom of God. And we give you the praise and glory. Amen.

—D. L. Moody

We Dedicate Our Children

Lord, I humbly dedicate and devote to you the children you have graciously given me. I pray that they would come to know you and be owned by you as your children—every one of them, from the youngest to the oldest.

Take possession of their hearts. Make them yours by adoption and spiritual revival.

Pour out your Spirit and your blessing on them, Lord. Enrich them with your grace, even in their early years.

Show their teachers how to guide them in the right direction, in the discipline and instruction of the Lord.

I have helped to bring them into the world. Make me an instrument to bring them into your church.

Lord have mercy upon them. Speak life to their souls. Let them never lack your grace or their portion as your children. Be a gracious father and a merciful provider to them.

And if you ever see fit to take them away, then prepare them for your presence and make me willing to turn them over to you. Or if you take me from them, my Lord, be a father to them when I am gone.

Keep them from this world's evil, and guide them through it in safety. Provide them with all good things in this life, but especially take care of their souls and give them treasure in heaven. Amen.

—Charles Simeon and Benjamin Jenks

A PRAYER FOR OUR AGING PARENTS

O Lord God, my heavenly Father, I bow before you to beg your blessing, grace, and mercy upon my earthly parents.

Do not cast them away in their old age. Do not forsake them when their strength fails, but have compassion on their infirmities and help them in all their weakness.

Do not hold their sins against them, but remember them in your mercy and for the sake of your goodness in Christ Jesus.

Grant them true wisdom and abundant grace. May you find their gray heads on the way of righteousness, and their souls ever precious in your sight.

Let goodness and mercy follow them all the days of their life. Let their last days be their best days. And the longer they live in this world, make them that much more fit to die and to live with you in everlasting life.

Be their guide until death, and in death their support and comfort. And when heart and flesh, and everything here on earth, fails them—may you never fail them. Be the strength of their hearts and their portion forevermore. Amen.

—Charles Simeon and Benjamin Jenks

Prayer of a New Parent

God and Father of us all, help me to realize most deeply what a precious trust you have committed to me, what a solemn charge I have to keep, and what an awful responsibility I have to sustain.

Give me faith to look to you for help, guidance, and a blessing in all my efforts to bring up my dear children in your fear and love.

I recognize my utter inability to guide and protect them in such a world as this. They have inherited the same fallen nature which I and all humans have inherited—the curse of original sin. We feel the consequence of the fall of the original covenant-representatives of our race.

So my children must be born again, or they cannot see the kingdom of God. O Lord, I feel and I own my complete inability to do for them so great a work. My deepest desire is that you would in mercy accomplish it in their hearts.

I also wish that my children may be instrumental in good to the souls of others, and that they would work for your glory on earth. Again and again I commit and commend them to you, to your grace, and to the compassion and tenderness of Jesus. Take them up in your arms, Lord. Put your hands upon them and bless them with a blessing which will never wear out!

Do with them, O Lord, as you will. We have no property in them. They are yours. We have consecrated them to you. But as long as you keep them here on earth, lead them in paths of usefulness and righteousness, and finally receive them to glory. For Jesus's sake, amen.

—Charles McIlvaine

A PRAYER FOR YOUTH LEADERS AND TEACHERS

Lord, who am I, that you should honor me by allowing me to help prepare souls for you ... even in a small way? But since you have shown your mercy and have called me to this work, help me always to remember that those committed to my charge have been bought with your precious blood. And so let my nourishment be to feed them with the sincere milk of your word, so that they grow.

Cause me to be like a little child. And by recognizing my own corrupt nature, help me to exercise my spiritual senses to discern the first evil emotions that may arise in young hearts. Help me to bring healing, like a skilled doctor. But may my students be drawn to obey you by the cords of love. And when I must offer correction, grant it may not be to show my authority, but purely out of the same motive from which you correct us—to grow in your holiness.

Keep me from being angry without cause. Give me patience, and teach me the meekness and gentleness of Christ.

You who taught the disciples to pray, pour out your Spirit of grace. Teach my students to desire and know how to call upon you by frequent prayer. Keep them unspoiled by the world. Help them to flee youthful lusts and to remember you, their creator. Train them up in the way they should go, so that they will not stray when they are old.

You set apart Jeremiah from the womb and called young Samuel. Set apart also these young people—in spirit, soul, and body. Preserve them blameless until the second coming of our Lord Jesus Christ.

You gifted Solomon with grace to choose wisdom over riches and honor. Incline their hearts to make the same choice. May they always renounce and triumph over the lust of the flesh and the pride of life.

Jesus, at age twelve they found you in the temple, listening and asking questions. Grant that these young people would also love to be in your house, and that they would have their eyes opened to receive the discipline of wisdom. If you choose to grant them years, may they shine as lights in the world. Or if you think it best to shorten their days, may they be equipped with purity of heart to sing eternal hallelujahs to you, the Father, and the Holy Spirit in the kingdom of heaven forever.

Grant this, O Father, for your dear Son's sake, Jesus Christ our Lord, amen.

—George Whitefield

Save the Children

O Lord Jesus, we pray, you who love the little children and bid them come unto you, help us to gather these little lambs into the fold. Direct their little feet into your paths in the days of their youth.

O how glorious it would be, if instead of waiting until these little ones are hardened sinners, and then making great, heroic efforts to bring them to you, we could mold by your power these little lives just now—that they never go astray, far down the darkened paths of sin and sorrow. Amen!

—Aimee Semple McPherson

We Pray for Others

May we spread your word globally

Pour out your blessing, Lord. Make the communities that call themselves by your name more like the name by which they are called, and even more devoted to the glory of God.

Give us a loftier devotion, a deeper consecration, a more obvious unworldliness, and a more conspicuous Christlikeness. And grant that the word you have entrusted to us may be spread throughout the world, that wisdom and prudence may be proclaimed to the ends of the earth.

Grant your blessing to our work, however feeble. We thank you that your strength is made perfect in weakness. May it be so in the ministries of your church. Spread abroad the knowledge of Christ's name, and may the kingdoms of the world become the kingdoms of our Lord and of his Christ, amen.

—Alexander Maclaren

Wake us up to reach out

Our Heavenly Father, we pray that you will give us more and more of the compassion of Christ. We read from the very beginning that he was moved with compassion, as was the good Samaritan when he met a wounded and dying man.

O God, give us the spirit of the good Samaritan! May we tell many of Christ and heaven. May we go to the homes of the despised and the outcast and tell them. O Spirit of God, come down. May we in the church find out who our neighbors are. And, O God, we pray that they may be filled with the Spirit of Christ, and that they may go and tell others the story of the cross.

We pray that there may be a quickening in the churches. Wake us up, that there may be a great work for us to do. And we pray that the day may be not far distant when many souls may be brought to Christ.

O Spirit of God, come down upon us now, that the hearts of your people may be made one, and that we may all glorify and honor Christ! May we be holy ourselves and consecrate to you our best service.

O God, may we hear the voice of Jesus! And as we listen may we be ready to go out and do his bidding. For your name's sake. Amen.

—D. L. Moody

A PRAYER FOR LABORERS

Blessed Lord! Help us to see clearly the spiritual reality: the harvest is so large and perishing as it waits for sleepy disciples to give the signal for laborers to come. Lord, teach us to look out upon it with a heart moved with compassion and pity. The laborers are so few.

Lord, show us how terrible is the sin of the want of prayer and faith, of which this is the token. Lord of the harvest, you are so able and ready to send them forth. Show us how you do indeed wait for the prayer to which you have bound your answer.

And then there are the disciples to whom the commission to pray has been given. Lord, show us how you can pour down your Spirit and breathe upon them, so your compassion and faith in your promise will rouse them to unceasing, prevailing prayer.

Lord, we cannot understand how you can entrust such work and give such power to a people that is so slothful and unfaithful. We thank you for all those you are teaching to cry day and night for laborers to be sent forth.

Breathe your own Spirit on all your children, so they may learn to live for this one thing alone—the kingdom and glory of their Lord—and become fully awake to the faith of what their prayer can accomplish.

As in every request, let all our hearts be filled with the assurance that prayer, offered in loving faith in the living God, will bring certain and abundant answer. Amen.

—*Andrew Murray*

Give me strength to share my faith

My God, you know my weaknesses, and you know how I want to overcome them.

Send your Spirit to help me in this warfare. Give me wisdom, O God, and the meekness of wisdom. Let the power of Christ rest upon me.

When I am weak then may I experience that I am strong. Teach me self-denial. And fill me with the love that gives life to all, and endures all, and overcomes all.

O Lord, help me to know how to share saving faith with the rest of my family, and how to live up to the duty I owe to the souls of those who live with me. Amen.

—*Thomas Chalmers*

A prayer for the nations

O Lord God, Paul may plant, and Apollos water, but you alone give the increase (1 Corinthians 3:6). We realize that without you we can do nothing. All our efforts are in vain without your blessing.

But Lord God, you hold the hearts of all your creatures in your hand, and you can turn them any way you want. Strip the hearts of this people from their idols. Turn their eyes away from seeing that which is worthless.

You can glorify yourself by making people monuments of your mercy, and you can glorify yourself by making them monuments of your wrath. Glorify yourself by making them monuments of your victorious grace. Open their eyes, that they may see that their feet stand on slippery places.

Lord God, will you especially have mercy on those who are not saved? Soften their proud and rebellious hearts. Do not be angry with them forever. Jesus of Nazareth, have you not died that they might live? Did you not become poor that they might become rich? Is your blood not sufficient to atone?

Then why have you hardened their hearts and blinded their eyes? Why have you withheld from them the divine influences of your Holy Spirit for so long?

Open their eyes that they may see that they are going down to hell as fast as the wheels of time can carry them. Stop them in their mad course! May a grievous cry be heard among your children on behalf of perishing souls, like the cry of the Egyptians when their firstborn were killed.

We pray not only for ourselves, but also for all nations, for those speaking every language. Grant that a countless multitude may be gathered in from the four winds of heaven.

And when the last trumpet sounds, grant that we may be caught up into the clouds of the air to hear the joyful sound: "Well done, good and faithful servant. You have been faithful over a little; I will set you over much. Enter into the joy of your master" (Matthew 25:21). Amen.

—Maria W. Stewart

Have mercy on our cities

Lord, we are often horrified by this poor world in which we live. We could wish that we did not know anything about it for our own comfort. We have said, "Oh! I wish we had a lodge in some vast wilderness." We hear of oppression and robbery and murder, and men seem let loose against each other.

Lord, have mercy upon the great and wicked cities in our land. What is to be done with these millions? What can we do? At least help every child of yours to do their utmost. May none of us contribute to the evil directly or indirectly, but may we contribute to the good that is in it.

We feel we may speak with you now about this, for when Abraham stood before you and spoke with such familiarity to you, he pleaded for Sodom. So we plead for our cities—even all the nations.

Lord, let your kingdom come. Send forth your light and truth. Chase the old dragon from his throne, with all his hellish crew. May the day come when the Son will rule the nations, not with a broken staff of wood, but with an enduring scepter of iron, full of mercy but full of power, full of grace and yet irresistible.

May it come soon, the personal advent of our Lord! We long for the millennial triumph of his word. Until then, O Lord, equip us for the fight, and make us to be among those who overcome through the blood of the Lamb and through the word of our testimony, because we "lov[e] not

[our] lives even unto death" (Revelation 12:11). We ask in the name of Jesus Christ your Son. Amen.

—Charles Spurgeon

Make us useful

Lord, make us useful. Let none of us live to ourselves, but may we work to bring others to Christ. May all those around us, coworkers and neighbors, know where we live. And if they do not understand the secret of our life, yet may they see the fruit of our life, and ask, "What is this?" May they enquire their way to Christ, that they may also be set apart for him.

Visit your church, Lord. May none of us imagine that we are living rightly unless we are bringing others to the cross. Keep us from worldliness. Keep us much in prayer. Keep us with the light of God shining on our forehead.

May we be a happy people, not because we are screened from affliction, but because we are walking in the light of God. Amen.

—Charles Spurgeon

We pray for the lost

Glorious Lord, you have taught us to pray for others. We cannot boast of what we are or what we have been. If we had received what was proper and deserved, we would still be in the gall of bitterness and the bond of iniquity. We would have been in hell.

Your rich, free, sovereign grace has brought us up out of the miry clay and set our feet upon a rock. So should we refuse to pray for others? Should we leave a stone unturned for their conversion? Should we not weep for those who have no tears and cry for those who have no prayers? Father, we must and we will.

Some couldn't care less about divine things. Get their attention! I pray they may be led to seriously consider their position and their destination. May thoughts of death and eternity dash irresistibly like mighty waves against their souls. May heaven's light shine into their consciences. May they begin to ask themselves where they are, and what they are. May they be turned to the Lord with full purpose of heart.

Others are concerned but hesitate. Some that we love in the flesh have not yet decided for God. Cast in your cross, Jesus, and tip the scale. Love irresistible, come forth, and carry by a blessed storm the hearts which have not yet yielded!

May we pour out our soul in prayer for the unconverted. You know where they will all be in a few years. Ransom them from going down into the pit! Look on those sinners, speak the word, and bid them live. Righteous Father, refresh every corner of the vineyard, and let the dew of heaven rest on every branch of the vine.

Above all, long-expected Messiah, come! The whole creation groans in pain until now. Lord Jesus, come quickly. Amen and amen.

—Charles Spurgeon

A PRAYER FOR MY CHURCH

Lord, bless your churches throughout the whole world. Clothe your ministers with salvation, and cause your saints to shout for joy. Grant that the time may soon come that all may know you, from sunrise to sunset.

Will you especially look down on the church to which I belong? Fire our souls with a holy zeal for your cause. Do not let us rest while souls are perishing for lack of knowledge. Increase the number who will be saved.

Bless our pastor with a double portion of your Spirit. Encourage his heart, and strengthen him inwardly. May he see the work of the Lord prosper in his hands.

And now Lord, what am I waiting for? Dispel every gloomy fear that pervades my mind, and enable me to hope in your mercy, and I will give you everlasting praises. Amen.

—Maria W. Stewart

Thank you for defending the poor and needy

O Lord God, as the heavens are high above the earth, so are your ways above our ways, and your thoughts above our thoughts.

Thank you that I am this day a living witness to testify that you are a God that will always defend the cause of the poor and needy, and that you have always proven yourself to be a friend and father to me.

Continue your loving-kindness, even to the end. And when health and strength begin to decay, and I draw close to the grave, then grant me your heart-cheering presence. Enable me to rely entirely upon you. Never leave me or abandon me, but have mercy upon me for your great name's sake.

I ask these blessings for all the poor and needy, all widows and fatherless children, and for the stranger in distress. May they call upon you and be convinced that you are a prayer-hearing, prayer-answering God. And we'll praise you forever. Amen.

—Maria W. Stewart

We Start the Day with You

At the Start of a New Work Week

We thank you, merciful Father, that you have raised us up again to see the light of another morning. We return again to the ordinary duties of life after a day spent in worship and service. Enable us to go forth with a real desire to execute your holy purposes and to live even more under the influence of your grace.

Keep our hearts and affections set on things above as we faithfully carry out our work, in service ultimately to you. May we go forth with a fresh impulse that motivates us to do your will from the heart.

Keep our thoughts on heavenly things. And may we serve you with a deep sense of our own weakness, looking to you for grace and strength out of the fullness which is in Christ Jesus. Help us remember that we are accountable to you for the talents committed to our stewardship.

We thank you for placing us in this little corner of the earth, favored with blessings. Thank you that we enjoy the clear light of Christian truth for liberty and security, abundance and peace. May the experience of your goodness as to the things of time make us call upon you more earnestly for the blessings of eternity.

Keep us in your grace for the day to come. Guard us against our great spiritual enemy. Support us in every season of temptation. And enable us to live in your faith and fear and love, under a constant recollection of your presence, with a continual desire for your favor. We ask all in the name and for the sake of Jesus Christ our great mediator and advocate, amen.

—William Wilberforce

You are close to us all this morning

Savior and Sun of the soul, shine forth this morning!

Cheer and gladden our hearts! Shine upon me and mine, upon all whom I love, and on all who love you.

Shine powerfully on my dear friends. And let us know that, though we are absent from each other, you are equally near to us all. Amen.

—John Newton

Thank you for your loving-kindness in the morning

Lord, what unutterable depths of compassion are covered by those words: your loving-kindness! Your kindness would be an undeserved mercy, but your loving-kindness is a miracle. You not only rescue, you embrace. You not only pardon, you are our advocate. And the robe of your righteousness, which is wrapped about your redeemed ones, is lined with the soft fur of your tender mercies.

And this for me, Lord, so vile, so unworthy, so often ungrateful and forgetful! What can I say to you for this?

In the morning, when all around are sleeping, Lord, waken my heart with your tender call. Uplift my spirit into true fellowship with you. Early hours with my God will sanctify all the day. In my quiet time with you, Father, so fill my soul with the sweet sounds of redeeming grace and pardoning love. Then through all the succeeding hours there may be melody within, and joy too deep and real to be disturbed or broken by any of earth's jarring discords. Amen.

—*Susannah Spurgeon*

May morning devotion linger

My mouth is filled with your praise, and with your glory all the day.

Lord, may this cry of my heart reach your ear this morning! Lips, tongue, and mouth are all empty at this calm, quiet hour, and I come to ask you to cleanse and consecrate them to yourself and your service, so they may be filled all the day with the sweetness of your love.

Far too often, my mouth is filled with the bitterness of earth's impure fountains. But now my chief desire is that only the bright streams of thankful love and praise to you should flow from it.

How seldom does the tender grace of early morning devotion last throughout the busy hours of the day? It is gone as the dew on the grass when the sun looks upon it, or as the fleecy cloud when the wind blows it away.

Why is it, dear Lord, that earth and earthly things have such power to draw away my thoughts and heart from the unseen but eternal realities which are so near and precious to me when I am alone with you?

Please teach me the blessed secret of abiding "in the shadow of the Almighty" (Psalm 91:1)! Amen.

—Susannah Spurgeon

Let me find you near in the morning

O God, your kind mercy has again preserved me through another night. You have defended me from danger, renewed my strength, and refreshed my mind.

But even if I am allowed to see the surrounding beauty of nature—the fields, a garden, the birds—I am undone without your presence, and without yourself.

So before I wade into the business of the day, Lord, allow me to find you near. I bow with gratitude and my heart overflows when I consider your favor. How often has the kindness of your grace cheered me, kept me from wandering, and encouraged me when I was ready to give up?

Even when I did not realize it, you prepared me for every day during these morning visits. You have given me a share from your treasury, a staff or a shield—though I often did not even know it. But that is what your compassion and friendship is like, my all-seeing, all-knowing, all-wise God!

And dear Lord, do you have yet another blessing? Are the warehouses empty? Dear Jesus, why should I so grieve you by doubting your faithfulness?

Be with me this day, and flatten every mountain of difficulty. Keep my soul from being stained by the world. And to you I give my praise, my God and my redeemer. Amen.

—*Benjamin Allen*

You offer a fresh page today

We praise you, O God our King, as we gather around your footstool this morning. And we will bless your name for all your loving-kindness and truth.

You are great in your goodness and good in your greatness. In you everything is found that can make your children glad, and we praise you with our whole being.

You have kept us while we slept, and we have awakened in safety. Thank you that this new day offers a fresh opportunity for devotion. You have turned for us a fresh page in life's diary—a page without blemish. Help us to keep it so.

Forgive the past, blotted with our failures and sins. We bless you for putting it away as far as the east is from the west, and for looking on us as if we had never sinned. We cannot understand love like this, but we gladly accept the assurance of your free and undeserved favor through Jesus Christ.

You have given us yearnings for a holy life; accomplish them by the grace of your Spirit dwelling within us and working through us. Enable us to do the day's work for you, for your glory.

Make us a blessing to those we come into contact with, that we may leave upon their faces and lives some traces of that uncreated light that we have caught from the face of Christ. We ask it in the name of our Lord Jesus Christ. Amen.

—F. B. Meyer

Make the crooked path straight, Lord

Our Father, let us hear you say to us as we step out into the day that you are with us, holding our right hand.

If only we can feel our hand clasped in yours, we will not fear the power of any enemy or the pressure of any trouble. Come nearer to us than the nearest. Speak in our hearts, saying, "Do not be afraid. I am with you. I will help you."

Keep us safe in the midst of the storm and guide us on the untrodden path. We are poor and needy and thirsty. Open rivers in the high places and fountains in the midst of the valley. Make the wilderness a pool and springs in the dry land.

Instead of being motivated by the love of Christ we are fickle and uncertain. We creep where we should fly. We stumble where we should run. We are often weary of ourselves—but do not be weary of us.

Some of us shrink from our life work, from unwelcome toil and irksome tasks, or from those we have to associate with. Enable us to see your plan and to trust you. You are working out your plan in our lives. Deliver us! Lead us through darkness by paths we have not known. Make darkness light before us and crooked places straight.

May we rightly use the discipline through which we pass and learn to distinguish your meaning in every trial. May we find the pearls at the heart of sorrow. May we walk the fiery furnace beside the Son of God and pass through the rivers leaning heavily upon his arm.

Keep us in your holy care and graciously provide. We ask it in the name of Jesus Christ. Amen.

—F. B. Meyer

We worship you this season

Great and gracious God, all sunshine is shed from your face. All the path of moss and bloom is the mark of your footsteps.

All music is the thrill of your heart. And all the colors—from blue to green, purple and saffron and rose—are but a reflection of your beauty.

On the coming springtime may the last shadow of winter's dreariness be gone. And may our hearts and homes be filled with the joy of heavenly spring!

—*Evangeline Booth*

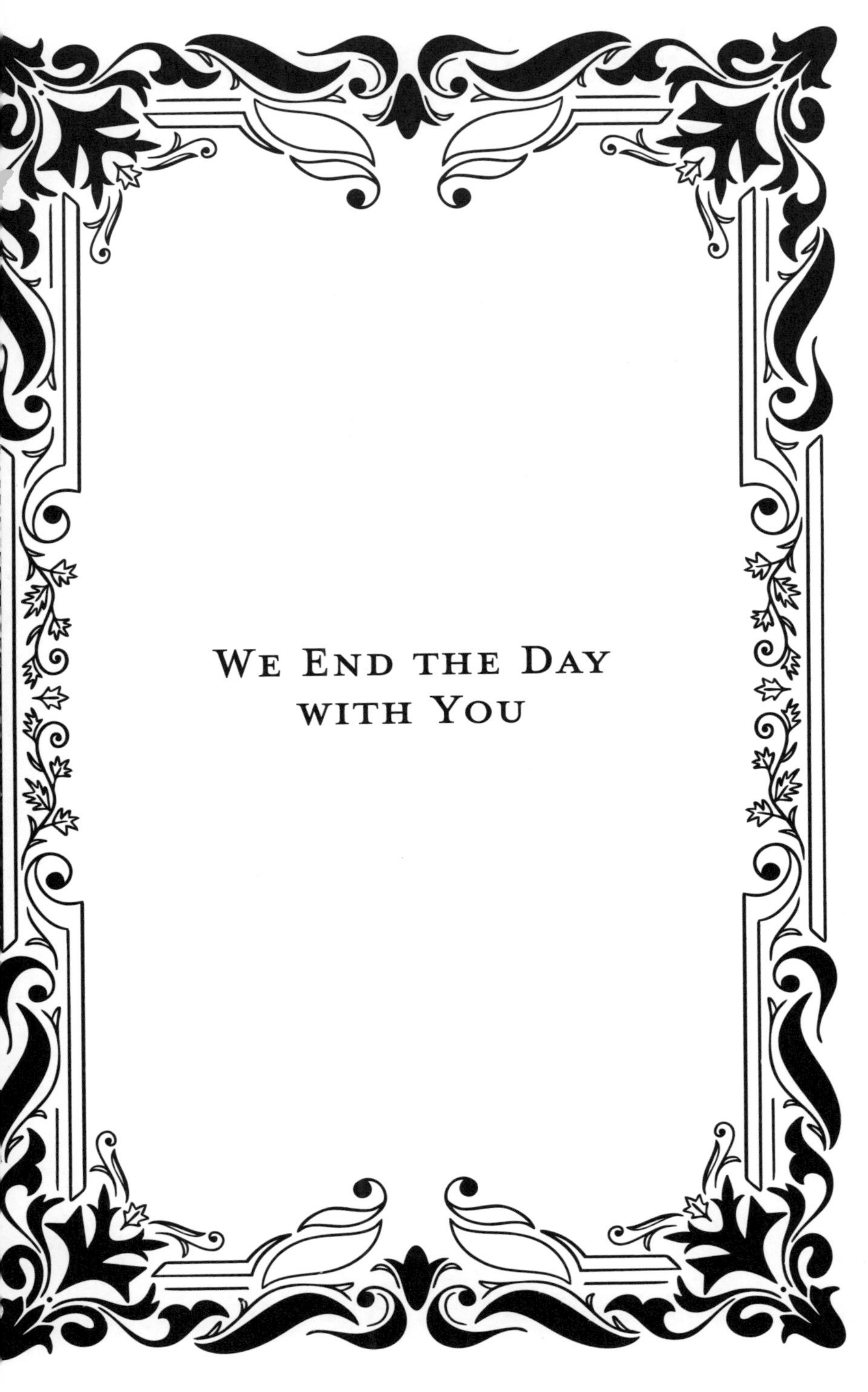

We End the Day with You

May we care the way you care

As we long for sleep to take the ache out of our weary bodies, so teach us to look for the touch of your Spirit to extract the restlessness from our hearts.

From our rest in you our thoughts look out upon the great world of men and women. We think of all the sin and sorrow sweeping over the world and bearing so many to destruction. Everywhere there is the groan of pain, the cry of the oppressed, the sigh. The world seems sad to us, but how much more sad to you.

Teach us to sympathize in your great pity, and whatever you have given enable us to count it a stewardship for others. You have given us gladness; may we make others glad. May we pass on to others the comfort with which you comfort us, and act as your interpreters.

You have called us to minister and witness, to go among others as our Savior went, bearing in our hands the balm of Gilead. May we not be disobedient to this heavenly vision. At whatever cost may we follow Christ in his redemptive purpose.

Teach us to pray. Pray in us by your Holy Spirit. May our hearts be filled with his deep yearnings and our lips become the medium by which he finds utterance.

We thank you for the Advocate before the throne who pleads our cause with you, but we thank you also for the Advocate in our hearts who pleads your cause with us. Make intercessions in us for the saints. Take us into the circle of divine supplication. When Jesus pleads for his tempted disciples may the Holy Spirit teach us to watch with him. And when he prays for his enemies may we pray also for those who use us.

Give us hearts large enough to sympathize with you, and may we give you no rest until you come to make right the wrongs of time.

Forgive the sin which your pure eye has seen in us today. Remember it no more, but may we remember it so as not to repeat it. Take us to your heart, Heavenly Father. Kiss us though we are stained with toil and sin. Cover us with the seamless robe of our Savior's righteousness. May we sit down at the table and may Christ the Door intervene between us and the fret of the world. Keep us safely through the perils of the night. We ask it in the name of Jesus Christ. Amen.

—F. B. Meyer

At the End of a Workday

Infinitely great, glorious, and holy God, thank you for the blessings of the day now behind us. May we lie down this night with a deep feeling of how much we owe to the longsuffering and loving-kindness of our God and Savior.

At the close of our best days there is much for which we have reason to be humbled in your presence. Enable us to feel our ruined condition without a Savior, and to fly for refuge to the hope set before us.

Help us remember that we are here for a short and uncertain season, that death and eternity are at hand. May we live therefore with our lamps burning, as those who wait for the coming of their Lord. May we be diligent in our Master's business, employing the talents and abilities you have given us for your honor. May we strive more and more to let our light so shine before others, that they may glorify our Father in heaven.

Grant that we may also be more useful in our day and generation. May we strive to serve you from a desire to do your heavenly will and out of a deep sense of the mercies which you continually pour out upon us.

Grant also that we may live more in peace and love one with one another, remembering that love fulfills the law. Help us to be the servants and children of the God of love, that we may be followers of God as dear children, and walk in love as Christ also has loved us, and given himself for us.

And now grant us this night, if it please you, refreshing sleep that prepares us for another day. We ask these and other blessings in the name and for the sake of Jesus Christ, amen.

—William Wilberforce

At the End of a Weary Day

Our Father, the day is past, and we come back to the calm evening hour.

Life is so feverish. Care and anxiety fret and weary us. The lusts of many things enter in to choke the divine seed. We thank you that we can climb up from the valley to this mountaintop where the stars of your promise burn and we feel the breath of your love.

O God, what would life be if we were not able to escape from its pressure and strife to you?

We confess our sins to you. We confide to you the causes of pain and annoyance which have made us hurt. Into your ear we can tell the story of our anxieties for ourselves and for those we love. At no other time does a child yearn more for its mother than during the first day of school. At the evening hour our spirits long for you whose heart is full of the gentle, welcoming love in which we can rest and forget and live.

We have been too self-centered today. We have forgotten that our best and happiest life must be lived in communion with the needs and sorrows and trials of others. Our own affairs, our growth in holiness, our little work for you, our circle of engagements—they have taken us out of the broad current of your life into the stagnant pool of our own.

Forgive us for the sake of him who pleased not himself and whose life was always laid down for others. May his love compel us no longer to live to ourselves but to him. May we find a balm for our own griefs and a solace for our own disappointments in sympathy and ministry to those whose hearts are breaking around us.

Bless those we love. Minister to them as we would, if we could be by their side—and better than we could, because your thoughts and ways are so much more tender and helpful than ours. Keep us safe beneath your wing during the hours of darkness.

We ask it in the name of Jesus Christ. Amen.

—F. B. Meyer

Looking back at the week, ahead at eternity

And now, Lord, when we once more come to the close of another week, grant that we may look back at what is past with gratitude for all the mercies we have experienced.

Help us to look back with humility, with an honest sense of all our sins, negligence, and ignorance. And may the solemn recollection that every succeeding week brings us nearer to our eternal home have a due effect upon us. As our allotted lifespan grows shorter hour by hour, may we daily be making progress on the way that leads to heaven. May each of us seriously examine heart and life, and may we ask ourselves the decisive question:

Have we entered that blessed path which will conduct us to glory?

Raise our low desires. Warm our cold affections. Overcome the reluctance of our unwilling hearts. And make us earnest in working out our own salvation, while we look to you to work in us to will and to work for your good pleasure. Amen.

—William Wilberforce

Gratitude at the End of a Week

Another week has passed, Heavenly Father. We come as your children with gratitude for the mercy which has brought us thus far and for the heaven of love that arches over us today.

We believe that you will not leave that which you have started until you have brought us to the end of the brief term of our life and we stand beside you on the threshold of the eternal Sabbath.

Many evils that we dreaded when we started this week have not come to us. Thank you. Storms have spent themselves outside the circle of our life. We thank you also that you have put into this week's life many blessings more than we dared to expect. Your mercy has been greater than our sin, your supplies larger than our need, your grace more abundant than the pressure of temptation.

Enable us to complete the unfinished work of the week, and perfect through us the unfinished plans. Bring us through troubled waters to a haven of rest. And as we started this week for you so may we complete it for you. We ask it in the name of Jesus Christ. Amen.

—F. B. Meyer

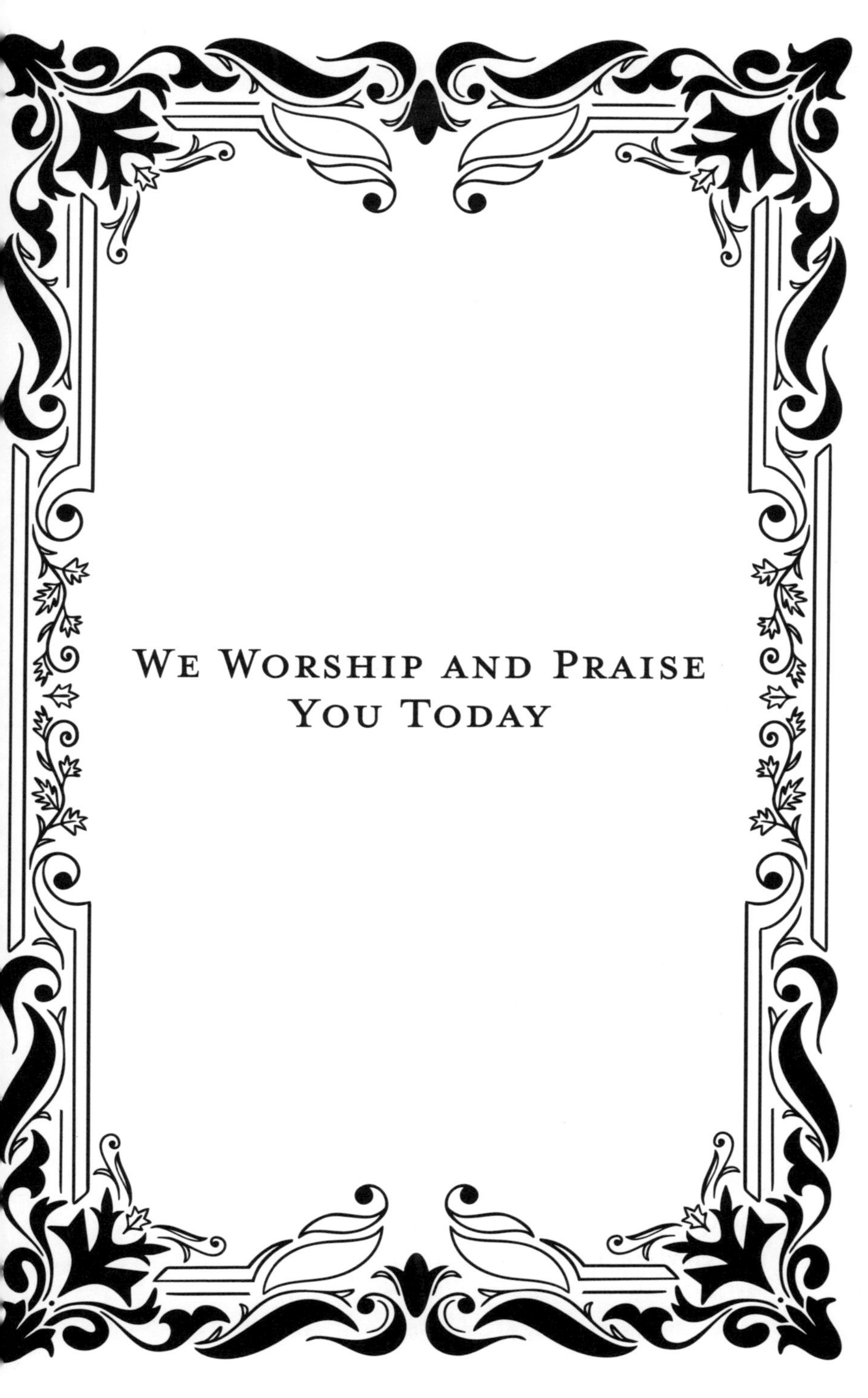

We Worship and Praise You Today

A reminder before communion: Who am I?

Lord, let me never forget the rock out of which I am carved. Let me never forget how I was shaped in iniquity.

Seth was born in the likeness of fallen Adam, a tarnished and transformed image. And that likeness has been transmitted to all his descendants.

You ordained this arrangement, this constitution, O God, and we cannot comprehend the rationale behind it. But you ordained yet another constitution. We cannot comprehend its rationale or legal principle, either.

You established that by faith in the second Adam, Jesus Christ, we are transformed into his glorious likeness. We are provided with his own everlasting righteousness.

The second constitution reconciles us to the other. They are parallel and they correspond.

And we say yes without reservation to the second constitution, because it so obviously displays the love that Scripture defines as your essence—the essence of God (1 John 4:16), along with the mercy that rejoices over all your works.

In this confidence, O God, would I now celebrate communion. In this confidence would I eat of the bread and drink of the cup, relying fully on the efficacy, that proven working of the atonement symbolized here.

Be with me, my God. Let me wash my hands in innocence, and so approach your altar. Enable me to pay my vows and verify the profession of faith I make here for all to see. Amen.

—*Thomas Chalmers*

A Group Prayer Before Worship

O Lord our God, from whom comes every good and perfect gift, make us aware of your presence in this hour of worship. And grant that whatever we most need for our inward life we may find here and now.

Draw our hearts to yourself and prepare us for better service. Help each of us to pass beyond the outward forms of worship and to come, in the silence of our minds, into the secret place of the Most High.

Flash your truth upon all our hearts and minds, help us in hearing and in speaking, and bless us each as we each may require. Receive our thanks for the individual blessings which we possess, and for the unspeakable gift of God in Jesus Christ.

Hear us, we pray, and grant us your presence and help now, for our Savior Christ's sake, amen.

—*Alexander Maclaren*

We dedicate ourselves this Sunday morning

On this morning of your day we offer ourselves to you, Lord of the universe, as disciples of Jesus of Nazareth.

He is the messenger of your will and your promises. He is the only true and living way to your eternal glories. We can be redeemed only by his blood. We can be taught only by his righteousness. We can be made and kept alive only by his mercies.

We are also followers in the faith of those believers who preached and spread the truth of Jesus, who held fast their belief amid the terrors of martyrdom, and who maintained a sacred courage of conscience amid the cruelties of a persecuting world.

God of mercy, may we never forget that every generation of believers has their own challenges, and that the life of a Christian is a life of perpetual vigilance. While we stay in the world we struggle with its vices and temptations, along with the passions and infirmities of our own nature.

Help us to remember, Lord, that Christians before us remained obedient not just on Sundays. Terrors of persecution hung over them every hour of the day. They were called to profess you amid never-ending dangers and difficulties.

In the same way, help us to remember that you require more than just a few sighs and prayers at the communion table. Help us to remember that we are also in perpetual warfare—just like those believers from the past.

And on a day devoted to celebrating the Savior's love, may we think of our unworthiness and helplessness. Remind us of our multiplied offenses, how forgetful we are of our duty, and how unmindful we are to the awful considerations of death and judgment and eternity.

On this day we acknowledge the gospel as our only remedy and our only reason to rejoice. May we see in our remembrance of a dying Savior that there is hope for the guilty who repent.

Renew us in obedience, and send us back to the world even more prepared to exercise our duties. And may this obedience last for more than a moment, but for many days, yielding abundant fruits of purity and righteousness.

As we sit together at the same table, may we live together as children of the same God and disciples of the same Savior. Remind us of that eternal feast which you have prepared for us. Help us to pull all our thoughts away from the vanities of a perishable world. Set our sights toward heaven, where brighter days await—where we will be purified from the imperfections of time, and present to the Father of Spirits the incense of a holier and spotless offering. Amen.

—Thomas Chalmers

Surprise us as we worship, Lord!

Lord, sometimes you surprise your followers with abundance. May it be so with us this morning! And if it pleases you, come into our assembly.

Although our petitions and praises are poor, compared with what they ought to be, grant your gracious Spirit to each of us. May we feel that it is no vain thing to wait upon the Lord.

We commit ourselves to your gracious care. Remember all whom we remember. Speak your grace to waiting souls, and in love rebuke the forgetful ones. Draw us all out of the mire in which we are too apt to walk, set our feet upon the rock, and establish our way. Amen.

—Alexander Maclaren

Help me to rejoice this day

This is the Lord's day. Help me, O Lord, to be glad and rejoice in the day which you have made! Oh let me live for Christ, and feel day by day the blessing of a will given up to God, and the happiness of a life which has its every circumstance working for my good.

Let me cast all my care upon you, God, and commit my soul also to your safekeeping. Keep me in perfect peace.

Make my faith firm and bright, so that death may seem small and not to be feared. Help me to trust you implicitly, so that with calm mind I may work while you let me live. And when you call me home, let me come gladly. Amen.

—James Gilmour

Help me to cultivate gladness

Filled with your praise. Abounding in thanksgiving. Brimming over with grateful love. So full of joy and rejoicing in God that "my tongue shall tell of your righteousness and of your praise all the day long" (Psalm 35:28).

This is how it should be, Lord, but sadly I have not glorified you this way. My heart has more often been troubled than glad, petitions have more frequently filled my mouth than praise, sharp and hasty words have escaped my lips, and the glory due your name has been less thought of than the passing needs of my sinful and selfish heart.

O Lord Jesus Christ, how much you have to pardon and how very far I am yet from being conformed to your likeness. A surly servant is no credit to his master, a thankless guest is no joy in a house, and a miserable Christian is abnormal in God's universe.

Lord, help me to cultivate gladness. Fill my mouth with praise and thanksgiving so there may be no room in it for anything else! I have your dear promise to plead when I ask this. You have said, "Open your mouth wide, and I will fill it" (Psalm 81:10). As the hungry little birds in a nest gape and clamor for the food they need, but cannot obtain for themselves, so do all the emotions of my soul long to be supplied by you, with the power to show forth your praise.

Through every moment of every hour of every day, may the consciousness that I am yours, and that you have loved me, stir my spirit to the constant melody of whole-hearted gratitude! You have said, "The one who offers thanksgiving as his sacrifice glorifies me" (Psalm 50:23). And I reply with joy: Yes, Lord! Your praise will ever be on my lips. Amen.

—Susannah Spurgeon

Give us boldness to worship

Our Heavenly Father, we look again to you for your blessing as we wait upon you. Help us to call our wandering thoughts in from the world—from its cares, its troubles, and its pleasures. May our thoughts be centered upon heaven and heavenly things, and may our hearts receive the word of God. Give us the moral courage to stand up and confess the Lord Jesus Christ in our homes or in our places of business, or wherever we are.

Lord, help each one of us that profess to be your disciple to be bold and fearless. May we not be ashamed of the cross of Jesus Christ, which is the power of God unto salvation. May each and every one of us be ready at all times and in all places to confess him who loved us and gave himself for us.

And we will give Christ the praise and glory in this life and in the life to come. Amen.

—D. L. Moody

A Sunday morning prayer

Lord God, now when we again return to the day that is consecrated to your special service, enable us to welcome its arrival. Help us to run the race set before us, that we may grow in grace, and have more and more our conversation and our treasure in heaven.

May we detach ourselves with thankfulness from worldly cares, business, and occupations, and set our affections on things above. Help us to recognize the vanity of human enjoyments, and may we pursue that good which is substantial and everlasting.

May we this day be filled with the spirit of the God of love. Root out from us all angry passions and evil desires. May we read your holy word today with seriousness and self-application.

May we pray to you both in public and private without wandering thoughts. Even in our recreation may there be some savor of heavenly things. Go with us to your house of prayer this day, and enable us to listen to your preached word with humility. Help us to remember that whoever plants or waters, it is you only that gives the increase.

Let us this day be full of thankfulness, full of heavenly affections, full of desire to do good to others. And may we enjoy a measure of that peace of God which passes all understanding, and of that joy that no one can take away.

We ask all in the name and for the sake of Jesus Christ our great mediator and advocate, amen.

—William Wilberforce

Praise to You No Matter What

O wondrous and glorious Triune God of the Bible. God the Father, God the Son, and God the Holy Spirit! You know all things. You are perfect in knowledge and infinite in understanding. I worship you, I rejoice in you, and I rest in you, knowing that you will never be taken by surprise or meet any emergency which you have not foreknown from all eternity and for which you are not fully prepared. I do not know the future, but you do. Things look very dark to me, full of foreboding and overwhelming disaster in business, and politics, and in world affairs. But you have known all these present perils from all eternity and have fully provided for them all. So I know that the ultimate outcome will be full of blessing and of glory, no matter how dark the present outlook may seem.

Hallelujah! Surely it is eternal life, to "know you, the only true God, and Jesus Christ whom you have sent" (John 17:3). Amen.

—R. A. Torrey

May the Spirit of Sunday Remain with Us

Heavenly Father, we are not tired of your sacred day. But we are tired in it.

We could wish that its holy hours might be lengthened, and its sacred activities might be prolonged. But since this may not be, may the spirit of this day remain with us so we may carry the lessons that we have learned, the praise in which we have joined, and the sense of your presence we have realized into the life that awaits us in the coming days.

Our hearts are somewhat apprehensive as we anticipate the contrast of this blessed day with the storm and strife of life. But you will be with us. We have your own assurance of your continual presence, and we know there is no step in the rugged way that you will not tread at our side.

We will not fear nor be dismayed. You are all the soul wants. Teach us the art of so living in fellowship with you that every act may be a psalm, every meal a sacrament, every room a sanctuary, and every thought a prayer.

And so may the week become lit with the light that streams from this day, and may the bells that ring be inscribed with holiness to the Lord. May we go up and down the aisles of daily duty in the spirit in which our feet have reverently walked through the courts of your house.

We ask it in the name of Jesus Christ, amen.

—F. B. Meyer

We Look to You at the End of This Journey

Let me finish well

Lord, you are infinitely lovely—so when will I love you without bounds?

When will I love you without the coldness or interruption which sadly and so often seizes me here in this life?

Let me never allow any creature to be your rival or to share my heart with you. Let me have no other God and no other love—but only you.

O God, help me persevere to please you. Help me tackle even the most painful or costly duties with a good attitude. Rather than disobey you, may I leave behind riches, friends, ease, and even life itself.

My service to you is imperfect and adds nothing to you. So how can I show you my affection? I will serve my poor brothers and sisters, members of your body. "For he who does not love his brother whom he has seen cannot love God whom he has not seen" (1 John 4:20).

O, crucified Jesus—in whom I live, and without whom I die. Put to death in me all sensual desires. Light up my heart with your holy love, so I no longer value this world's vanities but place my affections entirely on you.

And when my soul leaves my body, let my last breath breathe forth love to you, my God. I entered life not acknowledging you. So let me finish it in loving you.

Let my last act in life be love, remembering that you are love. Amen.

—Richard Allen

In my weakness I can look to you

O God, I go to prayer. Pardon, bless, sanctify me, and prepare me for a better world. My health is clearly not so good as it was, but I hope I regret it only because it indicates I am being called away before my work is done.

Sadly, how much more might I have done, had I been duly diligent and self-denying. But let me work at the eleventh hour. Lord, work in and by me.

Amidst all my weakness, I can look to you through Christ, with humble hope and even peace and joy in believing.

Lord, teach me what I do not know. Wherever I am lacking, supply me with the grace and strength I need. I cast myself on your precious promises, and claim your offered salvation. Amen.

—William Wilberforce

Help me be ready to live forever

Lord, our life is just a vapor that appears for a little time and then vanishes. Even at the longest, how short, and at the strongest, how frail. We may imagine ourselves secure—yet we don't know what a day may bring, or how soon you may call us to our last account.

Quickly our time will be just like water spilled on the ground that cannot be gathered up again. The days fly by, one after another, and we do not know how near is our last one. We do not know when our bodies will be laid in the grave and we will be called before God.

Yet how have I lived in this world, as if I should never leave it? I have not thought of my end. I have not used my time well, and been careless of my soul. I have neglected to prepare for eternity.

So in all fairness you may spring my last hour upon me like a snare. You may surprise me in my sins. But do not count my sins against me. Remember your tender mercy and loving-kindness.

Teach me to number my days, so I can apply my heart to true wisdom. Lord, what do I have to do in this world, but make ready for the world to come? May I be mindful and careful to finish my work before I finish my course.

In the days of my health and prosperity may I remember and prepare for when the world's enjoyments will shrink away. Let me never be afraid to die. And enable me to die to sin daily, that I may not die for sin eternally.

Help me prepare for a dying hour so I am not fearfully surprised. Prepare me for heaven and make me so ready to meet you at your coming, when you put an everlasting period to all my troubles and temptations, and exchange my present state of sickness and sin for endless glory. For the sake of my only Savior Jesus Christ, amen.

—Charles Simeon and Benjamin Jenks

Help us prepare for eternal life

Our Father in heaven, thank you for granting us long life. Enable us to yield fruit in old age. And may our last days be emphatically our best days.

While we await your return, may we day by day prepare—that mortality may be swallowed up by life. For Jesus's sake, amen.

—Lucy Thurston

I am fading—but you will never cast me out

Lord, I am like the flowers, settling into autumn. Grant that I may find the diminishing strength, which I must soon expect to feel, balanced by a ripeness in judgment and experience.

To be sure I have had more proofs of an evil nature and deceitful heart than I could possibly expect or conceive of years ago. I seem to groan under darkness, coldness, and confusion as much as ever. And I believe I must go out of the world with the same language upon my lips which I used when I first ventured to the throne of grace:

"Have mercy on me, O Lord, a poor, worthless sinner."

My feelings are faint, my services feeble and defiled. My defects, mistakes, and omissions too many to count. My imaginations are wild as the clouds in a storm, and too often foul as a common sewer.

What can I set against this mournful confession? Only this: that Christ has died and is risen again. And I believe you are able to save to the uttermost. And you have said, "Whoever comes to me I will never cast out" (John 6:37). Upon your person, worth, and promise rests all my hope.

But this is a foundation able to bear the greatest weight. Amen.

—John Newton

Life is short

O Lord, help us to always remember and seriously consider how frail, sinful, and mortal we are—even when we are in the best of health.

May we not boast of tomorrow or forget our dependence upon you. May we not abuse your patience with sinful vanities. And may we not smother our minds with needless cares, deceitful pleasures, or fruitless pursuits of this present world.

Grant us grace to pass the time of our sojourning here in your faith and fear. And help us to live righteously, soberly, and with godliness in this present world.

Help us to live as those who must shortly die. As those who are redeemed from death by the precious blood of Jesus Christ. And as those who must soon appear before your judgment seat.

Hear us, merciful God, for your mercy's sake in Jesus Christ. Amen.

—Alexander Viets Griswold

A PRAYER AT THE END OF MY LIFE

Lord of my life, you are my God from the womb. You have been my hope and trust from my youth. I was brought into the world by you. And you have patiently endured me, preserving me with loving-kindness and tender mercies.

I have seen many others snatched out of this life miserably unprepared for their death. But you prolong my days and add new mercies to my life. I pray that the lengthening of my days may be a real benefit. And as my life is prolonged, so may the work which you have given me be finished. May I redeem the time and improve all the opportunities and means of grace which you place into my hands. And let my age be good old age. Let the remaining time of my sojourning here be the best of all my time.

Though my sight is dim to the world, Lord, let my eyes be ever toward you. Though my ears are dull of hearing, let my heart be attentive to your calls. Let me hear your voice today. Let me taste the goodness of the Lord, and savor the things of the Spirit of God, and hunger and thirst after righteousness. And though my limbs are weak, and my strength will not serve me to travel as I have done, yet make me strong in the Lord—to do your work and walk in your ways. Help me on my great journey homeward, to my house eternal in the heavens.

Everyone alive eventually sees death. And the longer I have escaped it, the nearer I am now to it. One day I will certainly fall by it, and must every day expect it. My soul may this night be required of me. So let not my length of days tempt me to forget their end, or to put my last day far from me. But let me keep it ever in sight, drawing closer, that I may order all my concerns as one who is ready—waiting, watching, and preparing for the coming of my Lord. At your coming, may you find me ready!

And because I am old in sins as well as in years, weighed down with iniquity as well as with age, give me that godly sorrow for my sins. May they bring about repentance. You have saved many old sinners, O God; be merciful to me, a sinner. Put all my sins to the account of your dear Son and wash me thoroughly from them in the fountain of his precious blood.

Especially, merciful Lord, acquit and discharge me from the sins that lie heaviest upon me, and that make thoughts of death and judgment most painful. Let me know that I have found mercy, and that I may depart in peace, finish my course with joy, and be numbered among the redeemed and blessed of the Lord.

Through the tender mercies of my God, and through the all-sufficient merits of my only Savior Jesus Christ. Amen.

—Charles Simeon and Benjamin Jenks

In the End We Will Cease from Fear

We bless you for all your tender care our life long. Our first breath was yours, our last you will take unto yourself, and all the days between you will make precious by your presence and memorable by your redemption and deliverance.

Give us confidence, we humbly pray, in these solemn and gracious truths. Then our hearts will be quiet and will cease from fear. Then our life will be profoundest peace. Amen.

—Joseph Parker

Looking to the Evening of Life

Lord, prepare us by all the events of life for our great and final change. We do not know how soon it may come upon us.

You bless and build us up in many ways: through the Sabbath rest, the preaching of your word, prayer, and so much more. Use them in your wise and merciful providence to turn our minds from earthly concerns and prepare us for the everlasting life on whose borders we now stand.

And may your Spirit sustain and strengthen us in our last hours—when the shadows of the evening come upon us, when age and sickness arrive, and when human strength fails. Be the strength of our hearts, Lord, and our portion forever. Open the way for us into the everlasting kingdom of our Lord and Savior. Amen.

—*Henry Thornton*

Sources and Biographies

Benjamin Allen

The rector of St. Paul's (Episcopal) Church in Philadelphia, Benjamin Allen (1789–1829) was noted not only for his pastoral work but also for publishing numerous tracts and devotionals. Among other titles, he produced a weekly magazine, an abridged *History of the Reformation,* a *History of the Church of Christ,* and several works of poetry.

Sources Quoted

Memoir of the Rev. Benjamin Allen, by Thomas G. Allen (Philadelphia: Latimer & Co., 1832).

Richard Allen

Richard Allen (1760–1831) is remembered as the founder of the African Methodist Episcopal Church and as one of the country's most influential black voices of his time. Known as the "Apostle of Freedom," he organized Sunday schools, taught literacy, spoke against slavery, and worked tirelessly to promote the rights of black people in America.

Sources Quoted

The Life, Experience, and Gospel Labors of the Rt. Rev. Richard Allen (Lee & Yeocum, 1887).

Francis Asbury

Francis Asbury (1745–1816) came from England to the American colonies around 1771 and immediately began his life work as a traveling preacher. He would ride an average of 6,000 miles a year, speaking everywhere from camp meetings to tobacco houses to open fields. He was one of the few British lay preachers to remain during the Revolution and was eventually named bishop of the Methodist Episcopal Church in the United States.

Sources Quoted

The Journal of the Rev. Francis Asbury, volume 1 (New York: N. Bangs and T. Mason, 1821).

Clara Lucas Balfour

Clara Balfour (1808–1878) became well known for her work in nineteenth-century British temperance campaigns. Over the course of three decades, she traveled throughout Great Britain speaking not only on the dangers of alcoholism but also on the changing role of women. A mother of seven, she was also a best-selling author and article writer. In all her work she was recognized for her faith-filled perspectives.

Sources Quoted

"Life of Amelia Opie," in *Women Worth Emulating* (London: Sunday School Union, 1877).

Catherine Booth

As the co-founder of the Salvation Army with her husband William, Catherine Booth (1829–1890) was known for her energetic speaking ministry and spirited defense of women's freedom to share the gospel. Though she and William shared duties within the Salvation Army, Catherine herself would become a sought-after speaker and writer in the late 1800s. She even lobbied Queen Victoria for a "Parliamentary Bill for the Protection of Girls."

Sources Quoted

Papers on Aggressive Christianity (London: The Salvation Army, 1891).

Evangeline Booth

Daughter of William and Catherine Booth, Evangeline Booth (1865–1950) in 1934 became the first woman to lead the movement her parents founded. She spearheaded major efforts to raise relief after the 1906 San Francisco earthquake and received the U.S. Army's Distinguished Service Medal for support and relief work during World War I. She is remembered for saying "It is not how many years we live, but what we do with them."

Sources Quoted

Toward a Better World (Garden City, NY: Doubleday, Doran & Company, 1928).

Amy Carmichael

Though Amy Carmichael (1867–1951) worked in her family's Belfast street outreach ministry as a young woman, she was drawn to overseas missionary work after hearing Hudson Taylor speak at the Keswick Convention in 1887. From there she went on to work in Japan, Sri Lanka, and ultimately India—where she worked for decades, mainly with young women. She founded the Dohnavur Fellowship there and also published a number of inspirational books.

Sources Quoted

Lotus Buds (London: Morgan and Scott, 1909).

Things As They Are (London: Morgan and Scott, 1904).

Thomas Chalmers

No stranger to controversial topics, Thomas Chalmers (1780–1847) made his mark as a professor, minister, lecturer, and Scottish church leader. He helped establish schools and a church in some of Glasgow's neediest neighborhoods, and taught moral philosophy and math. His preaching was known throughout the UK. He was best known as an outspoken leader in the Church of Scotland and the Free Church of Scotland.

Sources Quoted

Posthumous Works of the Rev. Thomas Chalmers, by Thomas Chalmers and William Hanna (New York: Harper & Bros., 1848).

Select Works of Thomas Chalmers (New York: R. Carter & Bros., 1850).

Penelope Coke

Married to Dr. Thomas Coke, the first Methodist bishop, Penelope Coke (1762–1811) made a lasting impression of her own on those around her by her intellect, curiosity, and servant attitude. She and her husband established a considerable church-planting effort throughout England and Wales in the early 1800s. Her ministry within the British Methodist movement, however, was cut short by illness.

Sources Quoted

The Life of Rev. Thomas Coke, by Samuel Drew (London: Thomas Cordeux, 1817).

Theodore Ledyard Cuyler

New York-born Theodore Ledyard Cuyler (1822–1909) served in several churches in New Jersey and New York before being called to pastor Lafayette Avenue Presbyterian Church in Brooklyn—at the time, the largest Presbyterian church in the United States. He was an influential thinker, a prolific writer, and a friend to nearly every prominent evangelical of the day.

Sources Quoted

Newly Enlisted: A Series of Talks with Young Converts (New York: American Tract Society, 1888).

Jonathan Edwards

Often noted for his "Sinners in the Hands of an Angry God" sermon, Jonathan Edwards (1703–1758) played a key role in New England revivals during the eighteenth century. He is regarded as one of the leading theologians of the American Enlightenment period—which in some ways helped pave the way for the American Revolution. His popular books inspired many and are still read today.

Sources Quoted

Memoirs of the Rev. Jonathan Edwards, by Samuel Hopkins (London: J. Black, 1815).

Andrew Fuller

Andrew Fuller (1754–1815) is remembered as a Baptist pastor, theologian, and missionary supporter. In 1792 he helped found and promote the Baptist Missionary Society and sent out William Carey as their first missionary. His 1785 book, *The Gospel of Christ Worthy of All Acceptation: Or the Obligations of Men Fully to Credit and Cordially to Approve Whatever God Makes Known,* became a landmark of Baptist theology.

Sources Quoted

The Complete Works of the Rev. Andrew Fuller, with a Memoir of His Life (London: G&J Dyer, 1846).

James Gilmour

James Gilmour (1843–1891) served as a missionary with the London Missionary Society in China and Mongolia. During his time overseas, he often walked from village to village, dressed like a local shopkeeper, lived in a tent, ate only vegetables (so as not to offend), treated the sick, and shared Christ with anyone who would listen.

Sources Quoted

James Gilmour of Mongolia: His Diaries, Letters and Reports, by Richard Lovett (London: The Religious Tract Society, 1895).

Alexander Viets Griswold

As an evangelical Episcopalian, Alexander Viets Griswold (1766–1843) served several years as Presiding Bishop of the Episcopal Church in the United States, as well as Bishop of Massachusetts and Rhode Island. Around 1812 he published several papers defending the legitimacy of revivals or awakenings in his parishes. He and his wife Elizabeth had twelve children.

Sources Quoted

Prayers Adapted to Various Occasions of Social Worship, for Which Provision Is Not Made in the Book of Common Prayer (Philadelphia: W. Marshall & Co., 1836).

Memoir of the Life of Rt. Rev. Alexander Viets Griswold, by John S. Stone (Philadelphia: Stavely and McCalla, 1844).

T. D. Harford-Battersby

Thomas Dundas Harford-Battersby (1822–1883) served as an Anglican vicar and canon. Throughout his life he became deeply concerned with church unity and the deeper Christian life. Along with Quaker Robert Wilson, he was co-founder in 1875 of what would become the Keswick Convention—an annual gathering of evangelicals under the banner of "All One in Christ Jesus."

Sources Quoted

Memoir of T. D. Harford-Battersby, by "Two of His Sons" (London: Seeley and Co, 1890).

David Livingstone

Missionary-explorer David Livingstone (1813–1873) achieved huge popularity during the nineteenth century. His inspirational rise from humble Scottish origins, his missionary work and explorations in Africa, and his opposition to the slave trade made him a national hero in Great Britain. From Livingston Falls in the Congo to the town of Livingstonia in Malawi, numerous places throughout Africa still recognize him today.

Sources Quoted

The Personal Life of David Livingstone, by William Garden Blaikie (London: John Murray Albemarle Street, 1880).

Alexander Maclaren

During his 45 years at Manchester's Union Baptist Chapel and 12 years at Southampton's Portland Chapel, Scottish-born pastor Alexander Maclaren (1826–1910) became known as one of Britain's most popular preachers. He was a keen student of Greek and Hebrew, authored several books on the Scriptures, and served as president of the Baptist Union.

Sources Quoted

Pulpit Prayers (New York and London: Hodder and Stoughton, 1911).

Robert Murray M'Cheyne

Although Church of Scotland pastor Robert Murray M'Cheyne (1813–1843) died quite young, much of his influence continued after his death. His heart for God and dedication as a man of prayer inspired many—especially through his biography and writings published posthumously in *The Memoir and Remains of the Rev. Robert Murray M'Cheyne.* His Bible reading plan is still used today.

Sources Quoted

Memoir and Remains of the Rev. Robert Murray M'Cheyne (London and Edinburgh: Oliphant, Anderson & Ferrier, 1892).

Charles McIlvaine

Charles Pettit McIlvaine (1799–1873) grew up in New Jersey, attended what would become Princeton University, and served churches in Washington, DC, and New York. He was a chaplain and professor at West Point before the Civil War, with students that included Robert E. Lee and Jefferson Davis. Eventually he was appointed twenty-eighth bishop of the Episcopal Church and was sent by President Lincoln to London to argue against British recognition of the Confederacy.

Sources Quoted

Memorials of the Right Reverend Charles Pettit McIlvaine, by William Carus (New York: Thomas Whittaker Bible House, 1882).

Aimee Semple McPherson

Canadian Pentecostal evangelist Aimee Semple McPherson (1890–1944) had a lasting influence on the larger evangelical movement. She was an early pioneer in the use of radio to broadcast her sermons. Her Angelus Temple in Los Angeles was considered the first megachurch. And as the founder of the Foursquare church she worked to help build alliances among evangelicals.

Sources Quoted

This Is That: Personal Experiences, Sermons, and Writings of Aimee Semple McPherson (Los Angeles: Echo Park Evangelistic Association, 1923).

F. B. Meyer

London-born Frederick Brotherton Meyer (1847–1929) worked as a Baptist preacher and evangelist throughout

Europe, North America, Africa, and Asia. His preaching against drunkenness and prostitution had a marked effect during his day, and he was a longtime friend of fellow evangelist D. L. Moody. Today he is best known for writing more than seventy books, including commentaries and other devotional works.

Sources Quoted

The Epistle to the Philippians, a Devotional Commentary (London: The Religious Tract Society, 1912).

Prayers for Heart and Home: Morning and Evening Devotions for a Month (New York, Chicago, Toronto: Fleming H. Revell Company, 1894).

D. L. Moody

Dwight Lyman Moody (1837–1899) was perhaps the best-known evangelist of his day. From his humble beginnings as a shoe salesman, he ministered to Union troops during the Civil War and later went on to bring the gospel to thousands in the U.S. and Britain. He was also known for founding the Moody Church, two schools in his home state of Massachusetts, and the Moody Bible Institute and Moody Publishers in Chicago. The Institute still trains and sends out thousands of Christian workers today.

Sources Quoted

The Gospel Awakening, edited by M. Laird Simons (Chicago: L.T. Palmer & Co., 1877).

The Great Redemption, or Gospel Light Under the Labors of Moody and Sankey (Chicago: Merchants' Specialty Co., 1891).

Handley Moule

Handley Carr Glyn Moule (1841–1920) was an Anglican theologian and writer who served as Bishop of Durham from 1901 until his death nineteen years later. He was honorary chaplain to Queen Victoria and Edward VII, and also a proponent in the Higher Life movement (which emphasizes entire sanctification) and a speaker at the first Keswick Convention. As a New Testament scholar he wrote more than sixty books and pamphlets, and he supported the women's right-to-vote movement.

Sources Quoted

Secret Prayer (London: Seeley, 1891).

George Müller

Originally from Prussia, Johann Georg Ferdinand Müller (1805–1898) came to England in 1829. He began pastoring at the Ebenezer Chapel in Devon the following year, and with his wife Mary went on to found Christian day schools and Bible and tract distribution ministries. The Müllers were known for supporting faith missionaries worldwide (including Hudson Taylor) and for their ministry to thousands of orphans. The work they established continues today.

Sources Quoted

Jehovah Magnified (Bristol: The Bible and Tract Depot of the Scriptural Knowledge Institution, 1895).

Sermons and Addresses by George Müller (Bristol: W.F. Mack & Co.; London: S.W. Partridge & Co, The Book Society, 1898).

Andrew Murray

South African pastor and writer Andrew Murray (1828–1917) was known for his passionate writing, his emphasis on prayer, and for his promotion of world missions. The son of a Scottish missionary, he was educated in Scotland and the Netherlands, and pastored churches throughout South Africa. He was also a key figure in the Keswick "Higher Life" movement and authored some fifty books, including the classic *With Christ in the School of Prayer.*

Sources Quoted

Like Christ (Philadelphia: Henry Altemus, 1895).

With Christ in the School of Prayer, by Andrew Murray (Philadelphia: The Rodgers Company, n.d.).

John Newton

Though John Newton (1725–1807) captained several slave ships as a young man, he is perhaps best known for his conversion to faith in Christ, his work as an outspoken abolitionist, and for his hymn "Faith's Review and Expectation," better known as "Amazing Grace." He was a friend of William Wilberforce, whose efforts led to passage of the Slave Trade Act of 1807. He pastored at the St Mary Woolworth church in London until his death, and befriended evangelicals of all backgrounds—Anglicans as well as Baptists and Methodists.

Sources Quoted

The Works of the Rev. John Newton (New York: Williams & Whiting, 1810).

Phoebe Palmer

Influenced by the writings of John Wesley, Phoebe Palmer (1807–1874) and her husband Walter became a major influence within the Methodist and holiness movement. The couple often spoke at camp meetings, churches, and conferences throughout the United States, Canada, and the UK. Her books had a significant influence on the movement, as well—and on the effort to promote women in ministry. She edited *The Guide to Holiness,* a monthly magazine, until her death.

Sources Quoted

The Way of Holiness (New York: Piercy & Reed, 1843).

Joseph Parker

As a Congregational minister, Joseph Parker (1830–1902) was regarded as one of the most gifted orators of his day. His style differed from contemporaries and expositors like Charles Spurgeon or Alexander Maclaren, however, as he most often spoke extemporaneously, without notes or outline. His enthusiasm and spirit captured the hearts of his audiences, as did his approachable books such as *The People's Bible* series and the *People's Family Prayer Book.*

Sources Quoted

The People's Bible (New York: Funk & Wagnalls, 1887).

William Swan Plumer

During his lifetime, William Swan Plumer (1802–1880) was one of the Presbyterian church's leading voices. He pastored several churches in Virginia, Maryland, and Pennsylvania, and was also a seminary professor and author. While he wrote a number of commentaries, tracts, and pamphlets, he is remembered for books with titles like *How to Bring Up Children, Young Children May Be Truly Pious,* and *Truths for the People.*

Sources Quoted

Short Sermons to Little Children (Philadelphia: American Sunday School Union, 1848).

William Henry Ridley

The rector of Hambleden in southeast England, W. H. Ridley (1816–1882) was a prolific writer and pastor in the Church of England. He published a number of "plain" volumes for everyday readers, including *A Plain Tract on Confirmation, Sermons in Plain Language,* and *A Plain Tract Respecting Godfathers and Godmothers.*

Sources Quoted

The Every-Day Companion (Oxford and London: James Parker and Co., 1866).

Hester Ann Roe Rogers

Hester Rogers (1756–1794) was a writer and Methodist evangelist whose life and example were celebrated in a sermon by Bishop Thomas Coke. Called "The Character and Death of Mrs. Hester Ann Rogers," the account was later turned into a Methodist tract to portray her life as a role model for other women.

Sources Quoted

A Short Account of the Experience of Mrs. Hester Ann Rogers, Written By Herself (New York: T. Mason, 1840).

Charles Simeon and Benjamin Jenks

Though the two pastors never met, Benjamin Jenks (1646–1724) and Charles Simeon (1759–1836) are known as the co-creators of the popular updated *Prayers and Offices of Devotion for Families.* Jenks first published the volume in 1697, while Simeon substantially updated the work more than a hundred years later, in 1810. Another version was published in 1839. Jenks was a rector and chaplain, while Simeon was a prominent evangelical Anglican.

Sources Quoted

Prayers and Offices of Devotion for Families (New York: Stanford and Swords, 1850).

A. B. Simpson

As the founder of the Christian and Missionary Alliance, Albert Benjamin Simpson (1843–1919) was one of the most influential early evangelicals. He resigned a prominent position as pastor of Thirteenth Street Presbyterian Church in New York City to pursue gospel ministry to immigrants and the unreached. As preacher, theologian, songwriter, and author, he promoted world missions and a "fourfold gospel" of Jesus Christ as savior, sanctifier, healer, and coming king.

Sources Quoted

Christ In the Tabernacle (New York: Word, Work, and World, 1888).

Sadhu Sundar Singh

Sadhu Sundar Singh (1889–1929) turned away from his Sikh upbringing at an early age to follow Christ. While this ostracized him from his family, he also faced challenges at seminary when he refused to put off his traditional clothing. He went on to share the gospel with Hindus, Buddhists, and Sikhs throughout the Himalayas, India, and Tibet.

Sources Quoted

At the Master's Feet (London and Edinburgh: Fleming H. Revell, 1922).

Charles Spurgeon

The "Prince of Preachers," Charles Spurgeon (1834–1892) created a legacy which still exerts a sizeable influence on the church today—as he did while he was writing and preaching from London's Metropolitan Tabernacle. During his lifetime, Spurgeon preached to thousands and his transcribed sermons circulated widely. He held to a high view of Scripture, supported missionaries like Hudson Taylor, and often taught across denominational lines—despite his prominence in the Reformed Baptist tradition. He also built an orphanage and founded a Bible college.

Sources Quoted

C. H. Spurgeon's Prayers (London: Passmore and Alabaster, 1905).

Susannah Spurgeon

The wife of Charles Spurgeon, Susannah (1832–1903), also known as "Susie," outlived her famous husband by more than a decade. Although she always strongly supported Charles's ministry, she had a significant ministry of her own as well. She established a book fund for needy pastors in 1875, and wrote and edited several significant volumes. She was also active in outreach and even planted a church in Bexhill-on-Sea in southeast England, despite her own health challenges. Her legacy has been chronicled in several biographies.

Sources Quoted

A Carillon of Bells, to Ring Out the Old Truths of Free Grace and Dying Love (London: Passmore & Alabaster, 1896).

A Cluster of Camphire, or, Words of Cheer and Comfort for Sick and Sorrowful Souls (London: Passmore & Alabaster, 1898).

Maria W. Stewart

The first African-American woman to publicly lecture on anti-slavery and women's rights issues, Maria W. Stewart (1803–1879) pushed for nonviolent change based on scriptural principles. Her advocacy, eloquence, and evangelism raised eyebrows during a time when women were not expected to speak out. She is also remembered for her passionate writings on politics, equal rights, and everyday faith.

Sources Quoted

Meditations from the Pen of Mrs. Maria W. Stewart (Washington: Enterprise Publishing Co., 1879).

C. T. Studd

Cricket star-turned missionary Charles Thomas Studd (1860–1931) gave away an inherited fortune to fund Christian outreach efforts like the Moody Bible Institute, George Müller's mission, and the Salvation Army. But that was only the start, as C. T. then volunteered to serve as a missionary and evangelist in China, America, India, and Africa. He is credited with writing the poem, "Only One Life, 'Twill Soon Be Past."

Sources Quoted

The Chocolate Soldier: Or, Heroism, the Lost Chord of Christianity (Heart of Africa Mission, 1912).

T. De Witt Talmage

Thomas De Witt Talmage (1832–1902) pastored Reformed and Presbyterian churches and was one of the most well-known preachers of his time. After pastorates in New Jersey and New York, he moved to Philadelphia to lead the Second Dutch Reformed Church, and ended his pastoral career in Washington, DC. During the Civil War he served as a chaplain in the Union Army, and he also edited several Christian magazines. His sermons were widely published in newspapers nationwide.

Sources Quoted

Twenty-Five Sermons on the Holy Land (New York: J.S. Ogilvie, 1890).

Henry Thornton

Known as a respected and ethical economist, banker, monetary theorist, and member of Parliament, Henry Thornton (1760–1815) was also one of the early British proponents and supporters of the evangelical movement. He helped establish the Clapham Sect of evangelical Anglican reformers, and supported overseas missionary work as well as ministry to the deaf. He also pushed for the abolition of slavery with William Wilberforce.

Sources Quoted

Family Prayers (London: J. Hatchard and Son, 1834).

Lucy Thurston

Lucy Goodale Thurston (1795–1876) responded to a newspaper ad in 1819 calling for missionary volunteers—and soon found herself serving with her new husband Asa as a pioneer Protestant missionary to the Hawaiian islands. After their arrival in 1820, the couple set about building schools and churches on the big Island of Hawaii. She died at age 80 in Honolulu. Her vivid memoir, *Life and Times of Mrs. Lucy G. Thurston,* was first published by her daughter in 1876.

Sources Quoted

Life and Times of Lucy Thurston (Ann Arbor, MI: S.C. Andrews, 1882).

R. A. Torrey

Reuben Archer Torrey (1856–1928) worked closely with Dwight Moody in evangelistic campaigns, and also served as pastor of Chicago Avenue Church (today's Moody Church) and as superintendent of what would become the Moody Bible Institute. He would eventually preach in many countries worldwide, and toward the end of his life served as dean of the Bible Institute of Los Angeles—today's Biola University.

Sources Quoted

The Baptism with the Holy Spirit (New York, Chicago, Toronto: Fleming H. Revell Company, 1895).

The God of the Bible (New York: George H. Doran Company, 1923).

How to Obtain Fullness of Power (New York, Chicago, Toronto: Fleming H. Revell Company, 1897).

How to Study the Bible (New York, Chicago, Toronto: Fleming H. Revell Company, 1896).

How to Succeed in the Christian Life (New York, Chicago, Toronto: Fleming H. Revell Company, 1906).

Sojourner Truth

Born Isabella Baumfree, Sojourner Truth (1797–1883) was the first African American woman to be honored with a statue in the U.S. capitol building. Born into slavery in New York, she escaped with an infant daughter in 1826 and spent the rest of her life crusading for civil and women's rights and the abolition of slavery, as well as alcohol temperance.

Sources Quoted

Narrative of Sojourner Truth, by Olive Gilbert (Boston: Published for the author, 1850).

Stephen Tyng

Stephen Higginson Tyng (1800–1885) was a leading evangelical pastor within the Episcopal church. He was especially concerned with the needs of the poor in New York City and helped organize several social service programs. As pastor of the historic St. George's Episcopal Church in Manhattan, Tyng led noted banker and financier J. P. Morgan to faith. Two of Tyng's sons also became pastors. Dudley, his eldest, was an outspoken opponent of slavery.

Sources Quoted

The Christian's Own Book (Philadelphia: George, Latimer & Co., 1832).

Henry Venn

Rector in Huntingdonshire and chaplain to the Earl of Buchan, Henry Venn (1724–1797) was a pastor's son and Church of England clergyman with a heart for the poor and a successful preaching ministry. He often held prayer meetings in his home, and churches typically filled to capacity when he preached. In 1763 he wrote *The Whole Duty of Man* (later titled *The Complete Duty of Man*), from which some of this book's prayers are excerpted.

Sources Quoted

The Complete Duty of Man, or a System of Doctrinal and Practical Christianity (London: The Religious Tract Society, 1841).

Charles Wesley

The younger brother of John Wesley, Charles Wesley (1707–1788) was an English Methodist leader and hymn writer with more than 6,500 hymns to his credit. He studied at Oxford and eventually traveled with his brother to America—and later throughout Britain—to conduct evangelistic campaigns. In his later years he ministered mainly in Bristol and London. His songs are still sung in churches today.

Sources Quoted

The Journal of Charles Wesley, edited by Thomas Jackson (London: John Mason, 1849).

John Wesley

John Wesley (1703–1791) was known for his traveling preaching and outreach ministry, and for co-founding the Methodist movement. Wesleyan Arminian theology emphasized personal salvation by faith, entire sanctification, and social outreach. Though he remained an Anglican priest, his teachings and his efforts to train lay preachers formed the spiritual basis for many of today's Holiness and charismatic churches.

Sources Quoted

A Farther Appeal to Men of Reason and Religion (London: W. Strahan, 1745).

Instructions for Christians, by John Wesley (London: G. Story, 1800).

B. F. Westcott

Anglican bishop Brooke Foss Westcott (1825–1901) was known as a brilliant New Testament scholar and lecturer at Cambridge, as well as the author of a long list of scholarly works and commentaries. He had a wide variety of interests, from poetry and music to art and literature. He and his wife Sarah also had ten children, several of whom followed their father into Church of England ministries.

Sources Quoted

Life and Letters of Brooke Foss Westcott, by Arthur Westcott (London: Macmillan and Co., 1903).

George Whitefield

As an early Methodist and passionate evangelical preacher, Whitefield (1714–1770) is said over his lifetime to have preached to something like 10 million people throughout Britain and the colonies. He traveled tirelessly and used every means at his disposal—including print media—to promote and spread his messages. A major celebrity of his day, he crossed the Atlantic often and visited America from England seven times.

Sources Quoted

The Works of the Rev. George Whitefield (Edinburgh: Edward and Charles Dilly, 1772).

William Wilberforce

William Wilberforce (1759–1833) led the movement in England to abolish the slave trade. And as a member of Parliament, he also championed causes such as the Society for the Suppression of Vice, the Society for the Prevention of Cruelty of Animals, and various missionary groups.

After his conversion around 1784, he became a friend of John Newton—who counseled him to make a difference in politics.

Sources Quoted

Family Prayers (London: J. Hatchard and Son, 1834).

The Life of William Wilberforce, by Robert Isaac Wilberforce and Samuel Wilberforce (London: J. Murray, 1833).

George Williams

The founder of the Young Men's Christian Association, Sir George Williams (1821–1905) was knighted by Queen Victoria in 1894 for his community and youth work. A successful London businessman, he devoted much of his time to evangelism, and he created the YMCA in 1844 to give young men an alternative to the streets. A stained-glass window in the nave of Westminster Abbey still honors him.

Sources Quoted

The Father of the Red Triangle: The Life of Sir George Williams, Founder of the Y.M.C.A., by J. E. Hodder Williams (New York: Hodder and Stoughton, 1918).

Index of Authors